D1103948

SCIENCE SAFETY

for Elementary Teachers

SCIENCE SAFETY

for Elementary Teachers

E D I T E D   B Y   **Gary E. Downs**
Jack A. Gerlovich

David L. Fagle, ILLUSTRATOR

THE IOWA STATE UNIVERSITY PRESS / AMES, IOWA

Printed by
The Iowa State University Press
Ames, Iowa 50010

First edition, 1983

Library of Congress Cataloging in Publication Data

Downs, Gary E.
    Science safety for elementary teachers.

    1. Science—Study and teaching (Elementary)—Safety measures. I. Gerlovich, Jack A. II. Title.
LB1585.D68   1983   372.3′5044   83–4303
ISBN 0-8138-1641-6

CONTENTS

PREFACE

At the elementary level children learn best by *active participation*. Knowledge is gained by using fundamental learning processes essential to comprehension. Research by Jean Piaget indicates that an experientially based (hands-on) science program is preferred, together with an inquiry approach that capitalizes on the student's natural curiosities.

Some level of risk is inherent in many science activities. The problem is to determine an acceptable level of risk for all planned activities contained in the science curriculum. *Safety principles* enable us to choose between experiences that are unproductive or even foolish and those that enrich our lives and make them worthwhile.

Science safety for elementary teachers has been guided by the belief that safety practices are learned and habits are formed by following models presented by others. Therefore it is important all science teachers understand the implication their safety practices have for students who will learn from them. We recommend all teachers in elementary schools use this safety manual to practice, with their students, the essential rules of science safety.

Gary E. Downs
Jack A. Gerlovich

ACKNOWLEDGEMENTS

The authors thank especially the Iowa Department of Public Instruction for support in the development of this safety manual. In addition, the authors thank the Research Institute for Studies in Education (RISE) at Iowa State University for financially supporting the development and dissemination of the initial draft.

The opinions, findings, conclusions, or recommendations expressed are those of the authors and do not necessarily reflect the views of the Iowa Department of Public Instruction or the Research Institute for Studies in Education.

Elementary Science Safety Task Force and Authors

Gary E. Downs (Co-Chair)
Professor, Elementary Education
Iowa State University
Ames, Iowa

Jack A. Gerlovich (Co-Chair)
Science Consultant
Iowa Department of Public
  Instruction
Des Moines, Iowa

Norman H. Anderson--Certified
  Safety Professional
Risk Improvement Department
Employers Mutual Company
Des Moines, Iowa

David L. Fagle
Science Coordinator, Community
  Schools
Marshalltown, Iowa

Walter L. Hetzel
Attorney-at-Law
Ames, Iowa

Gil Hewett
Science Consultant
Area Education Agency 7
Cedar Falls, Iowa

Paul H. Joslin
Professor, College of Education
Drake University
Des Moines, Iowa

Clifford G. McCollum
Dean, College of Natural
  Sciences
University of Northern Iowa
Cedar Falls, Iowa

Kay Sonksen North
Teacher, Elementary Schools
Ames, Iowa

Harold Rathert
Science Coordinator, Des
  Moines Independent Schools
Des Moines, Iowa

Albert M. Sherick
Professor, Industrial
  Education
Iowa State University
Ames, Iowa

Burgess Shriver
Director, Math/Science
Des Moines Area Community
  College
Des Moines, Iowa

Milton Wilson
Consultant, Plant Facilities
  Unit
Iowa Department of Public
  Instruction
Des Moines, Iowa

SCIENCE SAFETY

for Elementary Teachers

1 Accidents: Statistical Background and Reporting

The major thrust of this manual is to make elementary teachers of science more aware of potential dangers in the teaching of science and the responsibilities in maintaining classroom safety.

An effective school safety program should contain three major components: safety management, safety services, and safety education.

Safety management includes planning, implementing, and evaluating programs throughout the school.

Safety services are best delivered in schools designed and built for optimal safety. Good inspection and maintenance of the total school environment are necessary; and adequate procedures for supervision of student activity and the handling of emergencies should be established and maintained.

Safety education involves provisions of meaningful learning experiences for students and inservice education for school personnel. The safety education program will be successful if (1) school personnel are enthusiastic; (2) the curriculum is well planned; (3) methods, techniques, equipment, and materials are up-to-date and effective; and (4) the procedures for improving the program are thorough.

STATISTICAL DATA

Employers Mutual Companies (EMC) provided the liability insurance coverage on approximately one-half of Iowa's 449 school districts during the three academic years 1977-1980. To assist in minimizing losses, EMC requested that the schools voluntarily submit copies of accident and incident reports and 88 schools responded. Among the schools in this group there was a wide variance of size.

There were 13,140 reports received during the three-year period. Of this total, 6,532 were from elementary schools. The

3

data base has been used for several analyses and the data group is large enough to be consistent and nonbiased.

Table 1.1 indicates the general nature of injury in elementary accidents and the relative percentages of each.

Table 1.2 presents data concerning injury to various parts of the body, a breakdown necessary for understanding accident trends.

From Tables 1.1 and 1.2 it is readily apparent that bruises and accidents to the head and face were the most frequent types of injury.

When the student injuries were coded, an approximate severity level was entered for each report. The results are listed in order of increasing severity in Table 1.3. It is apparent from Table 1.3 that most injuries were minor and required simple first aid only.

All accident reports were then coded as to activity type, the results of which are presented in Table 1.4.

The accidents associated with general science were tabulated in both the "Classroom activities" and "Activities off school grounds" classifications. Slightly less than 1 percent of all injuries were science related and most of them occurred during field trips. Injuries occurring on field trips were attributed to handling animals and slips and/or falls.

The largest portion of all accidents occurred out of the classroom. Often they occurred during activities that were less strictly controlled and supervised. Supervision for elementary students remains critical, especially during recess, gym and physical exercise, and activities off the school grounds.

TABLE 1.1. General Nature of Injury

Injury	Percentage
Bruises	41
Cuts	19
Sprains and strains	19
Fractures	11
Scratches	6
Concussions	2
Multiple injuries	2
Dislocations	1

TABLE 1.3. Types of Accident Severity

Type	Percentage
First aid not required	8
First aid	57
Minor medical	26
Medical	8
Major medical	1
Fatality	1 case

TABLE 1.2. Injuries to Various Parts of the Body

Injury	Percentage
Face	25
Head and neck	25
Hand and fingers	13
Leg	11
Arm	7
Ankle, foot, and toes	6
Eyes	5
Back	2
Shoulders	2
Multiple parts	2

TABLE 1.4. Types of Activity

Type	Percentage
Recess	59
Gym/Physical exercise	14
Classroom activities	8
Hallway movement	5
Horseplay	4
Activities off school grounds	3
Fighting	2
Entering or exiting building	2
Athletics	1

ACCIDENT/INCIDENT REPORTING SYSTEMS

Accident Reports

Accident data may be put to a great many uses. The information available through an effective school accident reporting system can be used by teachers, school nurses, custodians, building
principals, department heads, school superintendents, school
boards, school district attorneys, and many others.

Specifically, the systematic accumulation of school accident
and injury data will provide information upon which to base

- curriculums designed to educate children for safe living
- a realistic evaluation of safety program efforts on a regular basis
- changes needed in buildings, facilities, equipment, or procedures to improve the environment of the school system
- organizational and administrative improvements to strengthen
the managerial aspects of the safety program
- a strong public relations program, which will lessen public
demands for crash programs of little value if an unusual incident
occurs
- an assessment of the costs of accidents and injuries and
their relationships to the operating expenses of the school system

Individual accident reports can be useful for positive action
at each of several levels of the school system. Therefore, reports
should be reviewed carefully at each level through which they are
processed. Generally, an individual accident report

- may show conditions or deficiencies that can be corrected
immediately;
- can be used as a teaching tool;
- can strengthen staff interest in accident prevention activities through review of the accident by appropriate persons.

In addition, individual accident reports can provide important
information in cases involving teacher or school district tort liability.

Many different accident reporting systems can be developed.
Any system is good if it gives valid results in the simplest form
and with the least amount of effort. The answers to three questions will provide assistance in the development of an effective
accident reporting system.

1. *Which accidents should be reported?*

In most schools, a reportable accident is any school jurisdic-
tional accident which results in any injury to a pupil and/or property damage. (School jurisdiction includes school buildings,
grounds, travel to and from school, and school-sponsored activities
away from school property; the concept of property damage includes
damage to the school's own equipment, material, or structures.)

Every school system should require a report of some kind on

accidents defined as reportable. It is essential that the building supervisor knows of all accidents occurring within his or her school's jurisdiction. This sound practice offers some protection for the school in those areas where liability may be a factor. Most importantly, educational and preventive action can only be accomplished if it is known where and how all accidents and injuries are occurring.

2. *What information should an accident report form provide and what form should it take?*

No one report form will meet the needs of every school system. There is, however, a required body of information basic to the effective analysis and utilization of accident and injury data. Required information includes:

a) name of person involved
b) home address
c) school
d) sex
e) age
f) grade/special program
g) date and time of the accident, day of the week
h) nature of injury
i) degree of injury
j) cause of injury
k) location of accident
l) activity of person
m) supervision (who was in charge?)
n) agency involved (apparatus, equipment, etc.)
o) unsafe act
p) unsafe mechanical or physical condition
q) unsafe personal factor (bodily defects, lack of skill, etc.)
r) description of the accident
s) date of report
t) report prepared by (signature)
u) principal's signature

There is no model format. Keep it simple, easy to read, easy to complete, and provide enough writing room for a complete description of the accident.

Here are some considerations and timesaving ideas:

1. The form can be either mimeographed or printed, depending on the number needed.
2. Most schools use an 8-1/2 x 11 form; others use an 8-1/2 x 5-1/2 card. Some use both sides of the sheet or card. The form must be large enough to handle easily.
3. If several copies are needed, the use of printed carbon-impregnated forms is practical.
4. Paper should not be so thin as to tear when an erasure is made.
5. Some school systems use checkoff blocks for certain items.

This may or may not be a time-saver; it may be easier simply to write in the appropriate item.

3. *Who will use the form?*
The person in charge of the activity at the time of the acci-dent is the logical person to initiate the accident report. Plac-ing the responsibility on a third party who may have no firsthand knowledge of the incident would tend to make the report less us-able. However, reports from witnesses, particularly those individ-uals directly involved, may supply additional helpful information.

After the report is completed, it should be reviewed by the principal, and, as appropriate, by other school personnel, prior to forwarding it to the superintendent's office for action and filing. Examples of school personnel who may be able to use or contribute to the report are the school nurse; the custodian, particularly if there is an unsafe mechanical or physical condition involved; a department head; the school safety coordinator; or the safety com-mittee. It may be helpful to provide copies for some or all of those listed.
Monthly and annual summaries of accident report forms can pro-vide the information needed to direct the thrust of a school-dis-trict-wide program to aid in ensuring that students may learn in facilities that are as hazard-free as possible.

ACTION TAKEN OR RECOMMENDED TO PREVENT FURTHER ACCIDENTS OF THE SAME TYPE
If an accident happened once it will happen again--unless ap-propriate action is taken. An efficient and reliable accident re-porting system also includes provisions that indicate what action or method of prevention was taken locally and/or further recom-mended. In some instances, the action may not have been the direct responsibility of local school personnel. In those cases the re-spective person or group responsible for initiating proper action must be notified in the future. Procedures should be developed to ensure that corrective action is implemented on all reported acci-dents or incidents.
Identifying accidents that have the potential for serious or major loss is of paramount importance, and special attention must be given to those accidents with high loss potential. Many acci-dents do not result in serious injury but possess an enormous po-tential for predictive injury. Accident review, analysis, and the establishment of priorities for the correction and elimination of hazards is essential.

Incident Reports
Individual science teachers or department heads may wish to file records or reports on near-accidents, facility and equipment

defects, and/or unusual events which may have future impact on the participants of the science program.

The records or reports may serve a useful purpose in providing a safe learning environment or in cases involving teacher liability.

All incident reports should be written and processed with the same care and thoroughness as accident reports.

The value of incident reports in providing valuable accident prevention data for students and appropriate school personnel cannot be overemphasized.

CHECKLIST

1. Know the general nature of injuries for elementary students.   _____
2. Know what parts of the body are most frequently involved in injuries to elementary students.   _____
3. Be aware of the severity of accidents for elementary students.   _____
4. Know the types of activities where injuries are received.   _____
5. Use the district accident/incident reporting system (retain duplicate copy).   _____

2 Legal Liability

INSTRUCTION

Very young students are not generally thought to be negligent in behavior. However, as they approach majority age, they are expected under various conditions to assume greater responsibility for their actions. It is generally accepted that *children below age seven cannot be held responsible* for negligent behavior; *between ages eight and fourteen they may be held responsible*; and *beyond age fourteen they will be held responsible*. Professional educators are expected to provide greater levels of protection from injury for the very young student.

The current trend in liability cases is to have their outcomes decided by juries rather than by judges handing down decisions based on points of law. Teachers, as well as the state, the school district, the school board, and the school administration, can incur legal liability in a number of ways; however, only one is of interest here, and that is *negligent behavior*.

In all states it is the teacher, himself, who is legally responsible for the safety of his pupils. However, the courts have held that a teacher is liable for damages only if it can be proven that the teacher has failed to take "reasonable care" or has acted in an illegal manner. A teacher must foresee dangers, but only to the extent that any reasonably prudent person would. He may punish a child, within the legal limits set by his state, as long as the punishment is humane, is not excessive, and provided the pupil knows why he is being punished. In addition, a teacher must perform his assigned duties if he is to avoid being censured by the school district in which he is employed (Brown and Brown 1969).

NEGLIGENCE IN TORT LAW

Negligence in the eyes of the law may be defined as conduct that falls below a standard of performance established by law to protect others against an unreasonable risk of harm.

9

Whenever one is injured, it does not necessarily follow that
he will collect from another. Courts must first decide that
cause of injury. In making this determination, courts usually
pose four questions: (1) Did one owe a duty of care to
another? (2) Did one fail to exercise that duty of care?
(3) Was there an accident in which a person was injured?
And, (4) Was the failure to exercise that duty of care the
proximate cause of the injury? If it can be shown that failure to exercise the duty of care was the direct cause of the
injury, then the defendant may be liable. Relief may or may
not involve a monetary award (Hudgins 1976,54).

Due Care

Before liability can be incurred by a teacher, a determination
must be made whether that individual exercised due care. It must
be decided if the defendant reasonably foresaw a potential problem,
or should have seen the potentiality of a problem, and took necessary and prudent measures to prevent it. If he failed to exercise
that standard of due care, and if the failure was the proximate
cause of the injury, then the plaintiff may recover for damages
(Hudgins 1976,55).

Reasonable and Prudent Judgment

If the standard of care has not been specifically established
by statute, the actions or inactions of an individual will be measured against what a hypothetical, reasonably prudent individual
would have done under the same circumstances (Ripp 1975). Obviously, there can be legitimate and complex questions regarding the
course of action a prudent person would take under a given set of
circumstances.

One important aspect of the conduct of the reasonable person
is anticipation. A reasonable person is expected to be aware of
the foibles of human nature and be able to anticipate where difficulties might arise. Thus a pedestrian may not step blindly in
front of a moving vehicle expecting the driver to stop, and a
teacher may not direct a student to perform a dangerous experiment
without giving adequate instruction and supervision. The reasonable teacher must be able to anticipate the common ordinary events
and, in some cases, even the extraordinary.

Duties of the Teacher

The classroom teacher has three basic duties related to the
legal concept of negligence: the *duty of instruction,* the *duty of
supervision,* and the *duty of taking reasonable steps for the proper
maintenance and upkeep of all equipment and supplies used by students.*

Science teachers have responsibility for all three duties.
Students in classroom, field, or laboratory settings should not be
allowed to engage in an activity without first receiving proper instructions from the teacher. The teacher should include in such
instructions an explanation of the basic procedure involved, some

suggestions about conduct while performing the activity, and the identification and clarification of any risks involved.

One of the most frequent causes of an accident at school is the failure of personnel to instruct properly and supervise sufficiently. When accidents have occurred as the result of educators being derelict in their duties, then the injured parties may recover damages. On the other hand, *failure to instruct and supervise that is not the direct cause of an accident will carry no liability* (Hudgins 1976,58).

School personnel cannot ensure the safety of another from physical defects. They are expected, however, to take reasonable precautions in inspecting the school premises, *noting any dangerous conditions,* and taking necessary and appropriate steps to correct them (Hudgins 1976,63).

Contributory Negligence

A defense often used in a tort suit is that of *contributory negligence.* It holds that the plaintiff was the direct cause of the injury and thus has no suit for recovery (Hudgins 1976,56).

Comparative Negligence

Many states (thirty-five, and the number is growing) have repealed laws that provide for the defense of contributory negligence and have replaced such a defense with the *doctrine of comparative negligence.* This doctrine holds that when both the plaintiff and defendant have been found to be negligent, the degree of negligence of both will vary, to be determined by the courts, with damages awarded accordingly.

In Iowa, although the teacher, as well as others affiliated with the school system may incur liability, even while utilizing reasonable and prudent judgment, governmental subdivisions would be required under the save harmless provision (613A.8) of chapter 613.A of the Iowa Code to protect the teacher and pay any damages incurred. The only exceptions *to this requirement would be cases involving malfeasance (unlawful acts) or willful neglect.* These laws are explained in the following extracts and comments.

IOWA STATUTORY LAW
Tort Liability of Governmental Subdivisions

613A.1 *Definitions.* As used in this chapter, the following terms shall have the following meanings:

1. "Municipality" means city, county, township, school district, and any other unit of local government except a soil conservation district as defined in section 467A.3, subsection 1.

2. "Governing body" means the council of a city, county board of supervisors, board of township trustees, local school board, and other boards and commissions exercising quasi-

legislative, quasi-executive, and quasi-judicial power over territory comprising a municipality.

3. "Tort" means every civil wrong which results in wrongful death or injury to person or injury to property or injury to personal or property rights and includes but is not restricted to actions based upon negligence; error or omission; nuisance; breach of duty, whether statutory or other duty or denial or impairment of any right under any constitutional provision, statute or rule of law.

4. "Officer" includes but is not limited to the members of the governing body.

613A.2 *Liability imposed.* Except as otherwise provided in this chapter, every municipality is subject to liability for its torts and those of its officers, employees, and agents acting within the scope of their employment or duties, whether arising out of a governmental or proprietary function.

A tort shall be deemed to be *within the scope of employment or duties* if the act or omission reasonably relates to the business or affairs of the municipality and the officer, employee, or agent acted in good faith and in a manner a reasonable person would have believed to be in and not opposed to the best interests of the municipality.

For the purposes of this chapter, employee includes a person who performs services for a municipality whether or not the person is compensated for the services, unless the services are performed only as an incident to the person's attendance at a municipality function.

613.17 *Emergency assistance in an accident.* Any person, who in good faith renders emergency care or assistance without compensation at the place of an emergency or accident, shall not be liable for any civil damages for acts or omissions unless such acts or omissions constitute recklessness.

Liability Insurance

Iowa law allows school districts to purchase liability insurance to cover them against tort suits. The policies cover all employed personnel of the district. A great majority of school districts in Iowa presently carry liability insurance. *Liability insurance is a protection, but it should be regarded as secondary to the teacher's conduct.*

613A.7 *Insurance.* The governing body of any municipality may purchase a policy of liability insurance insuring against all or any part of liability which might be incurred by such municipality or its officers, employees and agents under the provisions of section 613A.2 and section 613A.8 and may similarly purchase insurance covering torts specified in section 613A.4. The premium costs of such insurance may be paid out of the general fund or any available funds or may be levied in excess of any tax limitation imposed by statute. . . .

The procurement of such insurance constitutes a waiver of the
defense of governmental immunity as to those exceptions listed
in section 613A.4 to the extent stated in such policy but
shall have no further effect on the liability of the municipality beyond the scope of this chapter.

Employer-Employee Relationship

Prior to 1967, under the *Sovereign Immunity Doctrine*, Iowa
public school districts could not be sued for torts committed by
the district itself or by its agents or employees. The doctrine
held that any government operation could do no wrong and therefore
could not be sued without its consent.

All this was changed in 1967 when the second general session
of the Iowa Legislature enacted Chapter 613.A into the *Code of
Iowa*, from which the following extracts were taken.

613A.8 *Officers and employees defended.* The governing
body shall defend any of its officers, employees and agents,
whether elected or appointed and, except in cases of malfeasance in office, willful and unauthorized injury to persons or
property, or willful or wanton neglect of duty, shall save
harmless and indemnify such officers, employees, and agents
against any tort claim or demand, whether groundless or otherwise, arising out of an alleged act or omission occurring
within the scope of their employment or duties. Any independent or autonomous board or commission of a municipality having
authority to disburse funds for a particular municipal function without approval of the governing body shall similarly
defend, save harmless, and indemnify its officers, employees,
and agents against such tort claims or demands.

The duty to defend, save harmless, and indemnify shall
apply whether or not the municipality is a party to the action
and shall include but not be limited to cases arising under
Title 42 United States Code Section 1983.

613A.9 *Compromise and settlement.* The governing body of
any municipality may compromise, adjust and settle tort claims
against the municipality, its officers, employees and agents,
for damages under section 613A.2 or 613A.8 and may appropriate
money for the payment of amounts agreed upon.

280.10 *Eye-protective devices. Every student and teacher
in any public or nonpublic school shall wear industrial quality eye-protective devices at all times while participating,
and while in a room or other enclosed area where others are
participating, in any phase or activity of a course which may
subject the student or teacher to the risk or hazard of eye
injury from the materials or processes used in any of the following courses:*

1. Vocational or industrial arts shops or laboratories.
2. Chemical or combined chemical-physical laboratories in-

volving caustic or explosive chemicals or hot liquids or solids when risk is involved.

Visitors to such shops and laboratories shall be furnished with and required to wear the necessary safety devices while such programs are in progress.

It shall be the duty of the teacher or other person supervising the students in said courses to see that the above requirements are complied with. *Any student failing to comply* with such requirements may be temporarily suspended from participation in the course and the registration of a student for the course may be canceled for willful, flagrant or repeated failure to observe the above requirements.

The board of directors of each local public school district and the authorities in charge of each nonpublic school shall provide the safety devices required herein. Such devices may be paid for from the general fund, but the board may require students and teachers to pay for the safety devices and shall make them available to students and teachers at no more than the actual cost to the district or school.

"Industrial quality eye-protective devices," as used in this section, means devices meeting American National Standards, Practice for Occupational and Educational Eye and Face Protection promulgated by the American National Standards Institute, Inc.

AVOIDING NEGLIGENT ACTS

Teaching personnel must be constantly aware of their duties as viewed by the courts. No student actions should be permitted without detailed instruction and supervision.

The following list of guidelines is intended to aid teachers in carrying out their duties and minimize their chances of becoming involved in any future legal proceedings:

Teachers should

1. protect the health, welfare, and safety of their students;
2. recognize that they are expected to foresee the reasonable consequences of their actions and/or inactions;
3. carefully instruct their classes and provide careful directions before allowing students to attempt independent projects;
4. plan activities carefully;
5. be careful to relate any risks inherent in a particular laboratory experiment to students prior to their engagement in that activity;
6. create an environment in which appropriate laboratory behavior is maintained;
7. report all hazardous conditions to supervisory personnel immediately;
8. keep adequate records covering all aspects of the laboratory operations;

9. be present in the laboratory to ensure adequate safety supervision;
10. be aware of and observe local laws and regulations that relate to laboratory activities in science;
11. provide written copies of safety guidelines to students, and periodically review such guidelines with them;
12. be consistent in their rules enforcement;
13. make and file written records of all accidents. These records should include statements from students who observed, or were involved in, the accident. These records will be valuable for future reference especially when dealing with minors and the implications of the statute of limitations (students may still file suit for an accident after they reach majority age).

CASE STUDIES
    The following case studies are not limited to the elementary science setting, but they give strong indication of the state courts' views of certain situations.

Cases in Which the Instructor's Conduct Was Adjudged to Be Questionable
    In the following cases, all of which took place outside Iowa, the science teacher was either held to be guilty of negligent conduct, or his or her conduct was held to be a question for jury consideration. If these cases had taken place in Iowa, and the teacher had been found liable, the school district or insurance carrier would have had to pay damages. This, however, does not eliminate the importance of teachers taking reasonable precautions to eliminate accidental injuries.
    An early case (*Guerrieri* v. *Tyson*, 147 Pa. Super 239, 24A 2d 468, 1942) raised the question of the circumstances under which teachers might be held liable for injuries that result from their attempts to provide medical attention to pupils. Of course, failure to obtain medical care promptly for an injured pupil may render a teacher personally liable if it appears that the pupil was in need of immediate treatment. However, if a teacher should attempt to administer medical treatment in the absence of an emergency, it has been held that he/she is personally liable where the treatment given results in harm to the pupil. Such was the situation in a Pennsylvania case in which two teachers, in the absence of an emergency, undertook to treat a ten-year-old boy by holding his infected finger under boiling water. The teachers were required to pay for the resulting injuries. The court pointed out that the teachers were not school nurses and neither of them had had any medical training or experience. Whether treatment of the infected finger, in the absence of an emergency, was necessary was a question for the boy's parents to decide, not the teachers. No evidence in the case indicated that the teachers were acting in an emergency.
    In *Bush* v. *Oscoda Area Schools*, 250 N.W., 2d 759 (1976), a female student brought suit for personal injuries against her

teacher, school principal, district superintendent, and the school
district itself. The student was injured when a container of methanol ignited in a classroom. A mathematics classroom was being
used for a physical science class due to crowded school conditions.

The room contained no storage or ventilation facilities nor
any of the other equipment usually associated with a science laboratory. Open-flame alcohol lamps were used in the science experiments because gas outlets were not available. Methanol was stored
in bulk in an old plastic jug which was allegedly damaged and
split. The jug and the lamps were kept on a counter in the rear of
the room. The student alleged that some methanol had been spilled
on the counter near a lighted lamp and, as she attempted to extinguish the lamp, there was an explosion and fire which ignited her
clothing and resulted in severe second- and third-degree burns to
her person.

The student claimed various acts of negligence including the
following affirmative acts:

1. leaving spilled alcohol exposed to ignition sources
2. failure to properly handle and store the methanol when open
   flame lamps would be in use proximate thereto
3. keeping the methanol in a damaged container

The plaintiff also claimed the following acts of omission:

1. failure to warn and supervise the students in handling methanol
   around flame
2. failure to train students and school personnel in the use of
   the fire alarm system and fire extinguishers
3. failure to have the fire alarm equipment in working order

The court held that the school district was immune from liability under the government immunity doctrine and that the superintendent was not personally negligent in any way. As to the teacher, the court held that her conduct was of such a nature as to
constitute a proper question for the jury. As to the principal,
the court held that he was not responsible for the acts of the
teacher but, as he was responsible for curriculum and class sched-
uling, he should have known of the dangers inherent in using the
mathematics classroom as a physical science laboratory and, con-
sequently, his conduct was also a proper question for the jury.

In *Simons* v. *Beauregard Parish School Board*, 315 So. 2d 883
La. App. (1975), the school board was held responsible for "ac-
tionable negligence" for a science teacher's lack of supervision
over a thirteen-year-old student's science exhibit. The student
was injured when he built a volcano using a firecracker for power
and visual effects.

Cases in Which the Instructor Was Adjudged Not Liable
An early case, *Gaincott* v. *Davis*, 281 Mich. 515, 275 N.W.,

229 (1937), which occurred in Michigan, raised the question of the
degree of care required by a teacher. The plaintiff was an eight-
year-old student in a class in nature study in the schools of De-
troit. The pupils in the class were required to care for the
plants, some of which were suspended in boxes. The teacher directed the plaintiff to water some of the plants, and, not being
tall enough to reach them, she took a chair from an adjoining room
to stand on. The teacher knew the child was using the chair and
that she was using a glass milk bottle to water the plants. The
child fell from the chair, broke the bottle on the cement floor,
and suffered severe injury by cutting her wrist on the broken
glass. An action for negligence was brought aginst the teacher.
It was held that in the absence of willful and wanton negligence,
the teacher was not liable. Willful and wanton negligence is that
which goes far beyond the scope of ordinary negligence. The court
also held that the acts of the teacher did not constitute even
ordinary negligence.

Teachers have not always been found liable in classroom and
laboratory accidents. In *Moore* v. *Order Minor Conventuals*, 267 F.
2d 296 (1959), a student was adjudged guilty of contributory negligence after he was severely injured in a chemical explosion. The
student, along with fellow students, had received permission from
the teacher to enter a laboratory to set up equipment for an experiment to be conducted later. While in the laboratory, the student
attempted to make a batch of gunpowder using a formula of his own.
He mixed potassium nitrate, sulfur, manganese dioxide, and phos-
phorus. An explosion occurred and he was seriously injured. The
student claimed negligence on the part of the school and teacher
because no instructions had been given to him with respect to
safety in the laboratory and no warnings as to the dangers involved
in mixing chemicals. The court held that the student's injuries
were the result of his own imprudent acts, and no award could be
granted to him.

In *Wilhelm* v. *Board of Education*, 189 N.E., 2d 503 (1962),
two thirteen-year-old students were working on science projects,
with the approval of the teacher, in a laboratory with the door
closed. After ten minutes, the two students began to play with
some chemicals in glass bottles which were on a laboratory shelf.
The students knew that the chemicals were dangerous. While they
were mixing and grinding the chemicals, the mixture flared up,
seriously injuring the plaintiff. The court held that the plaintiff was guilty of contributory negligence as a matter of law and
disallowed the claim.

In *Madden* v. *Clouser*, 277 A. 2d 60 (1971), two students had
been fighting over a pencil when the teacher briefly left the room.
One of the students threw the pencil as a male student was turning
around. The pencil went into his eye, resulting in the loss of
sight to the eye. The teacher was absolved of liability, since the
proximate cause of the injury was an intervening and wholly unfore-
seen force.

In *Demarais* v. *Wachusett Regional School District*, 276 N.E.,
2d 691 (1971), the Supreme Judicial Court of Massachusetts failed
to find a teacher of chemistry negligent by reason of alleged mis-
feasant conduct which resulted in an eye injury to a student who
was not wearing safety glasses. The court said that the standard
for teachers in public schools was liability only for their own
acts of misfeasance in connection with their employment. The court
found no duty to require the wearing of safety glasses. But even
assuming that the teacher was bound to require the wearing of safety glasses, the court held the teacher could not be held guilty of
misfeasance or mere inaction. The court further declined to hold
that the legislature had waived governmental immunity by enacting a
statute providing indemnification of teachers for expenses or damages arising out of negligence. In Iowa there is a law mandating
that students wear safety glasses under such situations.

The cases discussed give an indication of how courts view certain situations. However, the law is constantly being changed,
altered, or modified to deal with changing social patterns. The
current trend in negligence cases of this nature is in favor of the
plaintiffs and against the defendants.

Other Cases of Interest

Rand McNally and Company pays damages in school textbook mishap.
Rand McNally was ordered in 1980 by the U.S. District Court of Ap-
peals (Springfield, Mass.) to pay $155,000 to two former junior
high students who were burned in a flash fire while conducting an
experiment described in an eighth grade textbook, *Interaction of
Matter and Energy*. It is believed to be the first time in United
States judicial history that a textbook publisher has been found to
be negligent. Such a precedent decision could make publishers re
sponsible for students' misinterpretation of texts (*Publishers
Weekly*, 26 September, 1980).

Two thirteen-year-old female Paxton Center School students
were doing an experiment, independently of the class, involving the
calibration of an alcohol thermometer; however, they mistakenly
read the instructions for the experiment and added methyl alcohol
to a beaker of crushed ice over a lighted bunsen burner.

The students were successful in convincing the jury that they
were misled by the book. In an out-of-court settlement the teacher
paid $500,000 to one of the students, who suffered burns over 40
percent of her body, and $170,000 to the other student, who suf-
fered second- and third-degree burns. The teacher's insurance paid
for the liability damages. Those who paid premiums to the insurance company, of course, actually paid for the loss.

The importance of proper safety equipment. In October 1979 a
northern Iowa junior high school science teacher was conducting
class experiments resulting in the production of nitrous oxide
fumes. Since the room lacked exhaust hoods, however, the experi-

ments were performed by students along the windowsill with the windows ajar. As it was a cool day, the classroom doors were closed to prevent drafts from interfering with the efficient operation of the bunsen burners.

Numerous classes performed the experiment throughout the day. Late that afternoon the teacher (who held a Bachelor of Science degree in chemistry and had had professional military experience in chemistry) experienced symptoms of cardiac arrhythmia. Upon the teacher's admittance to the local hospital, the examining physician, from the classic symptoms, diagnosed the problem as nitrous oxide toxicity. In discussing the classroom situation, the physician stated that prolonged exposure to only 15 parts per million (ppm) of nitrous oxide in the room air can produce human toxicity symptoms. The prolonged exposure of the teacher probably resulted in the physiological problem. Student exposure for less than one hour probably presented little danger of similar reactions. (This case was described in a personal communication to the authors.)

It may also be noteworthy that the textbook had specified that performing this experiment in front of open windows was considered safe.

The nine cases described above give examples of actual teaching situations and incidents. Examples of this nature are more illustrative and forceful than a list of do's and don'ts. The nine cases can be used by all teachers as a yardstick against which their own behaviors can be measured.

CHECKLIST

1. Understand the following legal concepts as they
   relate to science teaching:
       Negligence
          Contributory   _____
          Comparative   _____
       Due Care
       Reasonable and prudent judgment   _____
       Tort liability   _____
          Save harmless provision   _____
          Insurance   _____
       Emergency assistance clause of statutory law   _____
       Sovereign immunity doctrine   _____
2. Be aware of state and local provisions related to:
       Adequate supervision
       Appropriate instruction   _____
       Equipment maintenance   _____
       Student protective equipment   _____
       Fire codes   _____
       Emergency procedures   _____
       Personal injury   _____
       Evacuation   _____

REFERENCES

Brown, B. W., and Brown, W. R. 1969. *Science teaching and the law.* Washington, D.C.: National Science Teachers Association.

Hudgins, H. C., Jr. 1976. Tort liability. In *The yearbook of school law 1976*, ed. P. K. Piele. Topeka, Kans.: National Organization on Legal Problems of Education.

Ripp, S. R. 1975. The tort liability of the classroom teacher. *Akron Law Review* 9:19.

3 Eye Protection and Eye Care

David L. Engle

It has been said that most of our learning experiences are developed through the precious gift of sight. Yet educators are often lax in protecting this gift.

Educators and future educators at the elementary level are responsible for the formation of the foundation on which a child must build his or her tower of knowledge. Teachers carefully prepare and present basic learning skills, but often fail to realize that the mortar binding these skills together is that precious gift of sight. They must do everything in their power to ensure that this mortar is not weakened, let alone destroyed, by a tragic accident that could have been avoided.

What can educators do as individuals to protect sight?

First, they must determine that all students are visually competent. They should also become completely familiar with what constitutes proper eye protection and when it is to be worn as defined in the American National Standards Institute ANSI Bulletin Z87.1-1979, and the *Code of Iowa*, Section 280.20, Eye Protection Devices for Students and Teachers. It is vitally important that educators be prepared in case of an ocular emergency and know what to do.

The *Code of Iowa*, Section 280.20, deals with eye protection for use in classroom activities; it is very explicit and leaves no room for guessing or omitting. Proper eye protection shall be worn under the conditions specified in the law.

Some elementary teachers will look at the requirements of this law and believe that they do not apply to their classroom activities. These teachers fail to take into consideration the science subjects (and perhaps the industrial arts subjects) that are covered in the classroom. What about the various chemicals that are used? How will they affect the eye(s) if they should splash into the eye(s)?

The law is specific in saying that the eye protection that

shall be used must meet the standards set forth by the American
National Standards Institute ANSI Bulletin Z87.1-1979. There is a
"grandfather clause" that allows eye protection devices that have
met the Z87.1-1968 standards to be used until they wear out.

PROPER EYE PROTECTION

Splash Goggle: Flexible
      The type of eye protection that is recommended for use in the
elementary class is the type known as a "splash goggle: flexible."
This eye protector is sometimes called a "chemistry goggle." This
type of goggle is made by some manufacturers to fit the elementary
student. Figure 3.1 shows this type of goggle.
      Below is listed the identifying information that educators
should know in order to be sure that the eye protective device
meets the ANSI standards.

1. The lens shall bear the manufacturer's trademark.
2. The frame shall bear the manufacturer's trademark.
3. The frame shall bear the "Z87" logo. This indicates that it
    meets the Z87.1-1979 ANSI standards. The Z87.1-1968 standards
    may still be used. The "Z87" logo is not required on these
    goggles, but all other trademarks shall be used.
4. Frames shall have hooded ventilation.
5. Important:
    Cellulose nitrate or materials having flammability characteris-
    tics approximating those of cellulose *shall not be used*.

      It is best that each student have his/her own splash goggles;
but this is not always possible. If this were possible, the teacher would not have to worry about disinfection of the eye protective
devices.
      If students share eye protective equipment, teachers should
observe the following ANSI-Z87.1-1979 6.4.3.2 disinfection procedure:

1. Thoroughly clean all surfaces with soap or suitable detergent
    and warm water.
2. Carefully rinse all traces of soap or detergent.
3. Completely immerse the protector for 10 minutes in a solution
    of modified phenol, hypochlorite, quaternary ammonium compound,
    or other disinfection reagent, in a strength specified by the
    manufacturer of the protective equipment, at a room temperature
    of 20°C (68°F).
4. Remove protector from solution and suspend in a clean dry place
    for air drying at room temperature, or with heated air.
5. Do not rinse because this will remove the residual effect.
6. Ultraviolet disinfecting equipment may be utilized in conjunc-
    tion with the preceding washing procedure, when such equipment
    can be demonstrated to provide comparable disinfection.

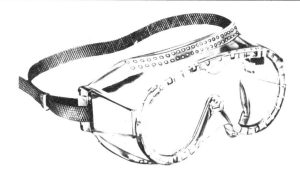

FIG. 3.1. Sellstrom Goggle. Splash goggle--flexible; sometimes called "chemistry goggle."

7. Spray type disinfection solutions and bactericides may be utilized when such pressurized spray solutions can be demonstrated to provide comparable disinfection with the immersion procedure outlined above.

Disinfection may also be accomplished by utilizing approved irradiation or ozone cabinets.

The lenses for the splash goggle may be acquired with an antifogging coating or the teacher may apply an antifogging compound after each disinfection.

Also remember that splash goggles should be kept clean and in good repair at all times. They should be stored in clean, dustproof containers.

Contact Lenses

The American Academy of Ophthalmology has published the following policy statement concerning the use of contact lenses:

> Safety or medical personnel should not disqualify an employee who can achieve visual rehabilitation by contact lenses, either in job placement or return to a job category. Rather, employees whose central and peripheral vision can be increased by the wearing of contact lenses as contrasted to spectacle lenses, should be encouraged to wear contact lenses in industrial environments, in combination with appropriate industrial safety eyewear, except where there is likelihood of injury from intense heat, massive chemical splash, highly particulate atmosphere, or where federal regulations prohibit such use. Safety and/or medical personnel should determine on an individual basis the advisability of wearing contact lenses in jobs that require unique visual performance, based on consideration of OSHA and NIOSHA recommendations.

With the advent of soft contact lenses, gas permeable lenses, and extended-wear contacts, the popularity of this form of visual correction is growing rapidly. Now, more than 14 million Americans are choosing this form of visual correction. Over 50 percent of these contact lens wearers are under twenty-four years of age with a higher and higher percentage in the elementary grades. Educators must be especially alert for these students and be certain that they are adequately protected from flying objects and splash.

ANSI-Z87.1-1979 4.3 Contact Lenses.
Contact lenses, of themselves, do not provide eye protection in the industrial sense and shall not be worn in a hazardous environment without appropriate covering eye wear.
A. *Splash cover goggles.*
When splash cover goggles are used with contact lenses there should be enough ventilation ports on each side of the frame to allow enough oxygen to reach the eyes thus reducing lens irritation.

If educators plan to do other experiments in the classroom, there are other eye protective devices that can be used. It is best that educators consult someone who has an understanding of the ANSI standards and can recommend the proper type of eye protection. Listed below are two important parts of the ANSI standards that teachers should be aware of.

ANSI-Z87.1-1979 6.3.3.3.4 Special-purpose Lenses.
Variable-tint plano (noncorrective) and corrective-protective (Rx) photoropic (photochromic) lenses are not allowed for indoor application and are only allowable for outdoor tasks which do not involve hazardous ultraviolet or infrared radiation, or both. All photoropic lenses shall be distinctly and permanently marked with the symbol "V", as well as the manufacturer's trademark.

ANSI-Z136.1-1976 Laser Protection.
1. Persons must be furnished with laser eye protection if they are working with, or around, where a laser is being used. The protection must be for the specific wavelength of the laser and be of optical density adequate for the energy involved.
2. All laser protective eye wear must bear a label identifying the following:
a) Laser wavelength
b) Optical density
c) Visible light transmission
3. For laser protection information refer to the manufacturer's specifications as to the laser eye protection that is necessary for the laser being used.
4. For more information on laser protection, refer to the American National Standards Institute Bulletin for safe use of lasers, ANSI-Z136.1-1976.

Remember, teachers and administrators are subject to litigation in tort liability if a student suffers an eye injury or other injury as a result of not wearing approved eye protection at the appropriate times.

OCULAR EMERGENCIES--WHAT TO DO

Protection is a must and will prevent or at least significantly minimize eye injuries, but this is not sufficient. Teachers must be prepared to render emergency treatment on a moment's notice. The school nurse may not be available. Remember, what is done in the first few minutes may make a difference between permanent visual impairment or possibly even blindness.

Equipment and Information Necessary to Meet Ocular Emergencies:

1. posted phone number of the nearest ophthalmologist or hospital--call first
2. posted phone number for emergency transportation
3. posted phone number of the University of Iowa Poison Control Center
4. Approved eye-wash fountain
5. Q-tips
6. ample supply of sterile eye patches
7. ample supply of surgical tape
8. eyecups

Types of Ocular Injuries

Injury to the eyelid--contusion or laceration:
1. Call ophthalmologist or hospital.
2. Stop hemorrhage: gentle direct pressure with sterile eye pads and cold compress or ice.
3. Apply sterile pressure patch.
4. Continue cold compress or ice to reduce swelling, hemorrhage, and pain.
5. Transport for medical attention with patient in supine position, head slightly elevated.

Injury to the eye--contusion:
1. Call ophthalmologist or hospital.
2. Do not irrigate.
3. Apply dry sterile dressing; do not use pressure patch.
4. Apply ice or cold compress to reduce hemorrhage.
5. The structure of the eye may be torn or ruptured. You may wish to cover the eye to reduce eye movement.
6. Transport as soon as possible to hospital with patient supine, head slightly elevated.

Injury to the eye--penetrating:
1. Call ophthalmologist or hospital.
2. Do not irrigate.
3. Do not attempt to remove object.

4. Cover both eyes with loose sterile eye patches to reduce movement and infection. DO NOT PRESSURE BANDAGE.
5. Apply cold compress to reduce hemorrhage.
6. Keep patient quiet.

Chemical burn to the eye--only true emergency: Acids cause serious damage immediately. Alkalines (bases), however, are the most serious, with a slower reaction time. It is sometimes hours to days before complete reaction occurs.
1. Invert lid if possible over Q-tip.
2. Irrigate profusely for 10-15 minutes in approved eye-wash fountain.
3. Call ophthalmologist or hospital.
4. While irrigating, have someone else call the local or state Poison Control Center. Tell them what chemical entered the eye and you will be informed of probable severity of the injury and the necessary antidote.
5. Transport immediately in supine position to ophthalmologist or hospital.
6. Continue diluting the chemical by use of eyecup.

REMEMBER, chemical burns to the eyes are the only true emergency. Prompt action is necessary--IRRIGATE, IRRIGATE, IRRIGATE!

USE OF BLINDFOLDS
Some experiments are conducted in the elementary classroom that require the pupil to be blindfolded. It is possible to transmit skin and eye diseases when students share blindfolds. In the past, very little attention has been paid to a disinfecting procedure that should be used after each pupil finishes the experiment. The authors recommend that each student provide his or her own blindfold; or that each blindfold be properly washed before it is worn by another student.

OTHER RECOMMENDATIONS
It is recommended that

● all students enrolling have a complete eye examination;
● yearly eye examinations be conducted; with the rapid growth of children, visual errors can develop in seemingly short periods of time;
● at the very minimum a written statement from the student's eye care practitioner should be required stating that the student is visually competent, or at the least, a visual screening should be performed by the school nurse on an annual basis.

Teachers should be aware of the symptoms manifested by students with impaired visual efficiency. Obtain these informational materials from local eye care practitioners or state optometric associations.

Teachers should ascertain the names of all students required to wear corrective lenses--whether spectacles or contact lenses-- and determine from the parents or eye care practitioner as to when the corrective eye wear is to be worn in the educational environment.

Most state laws require that all children entering school must have a complete physical check, dental check, and current immunization, but they fail to specify a complete visual examination. One of every four school-age children has a visual problem that requires some form of visual correction.

CHECKLIST

1. Be aware of the appropriate ANSI specifications and use of proper eye protective devices. _____
2. Know how to identify eye protective equipment that meets ANSI standards. _____
3. Know how to properly disinfect eye protective devices. _____
4. Know that contact lenses do not provide adequate eye protection and must not be worn in a hazardous environment without appropriate cover goggles. _____
5. Know the procedures to follow in ocular emergencies. _____
6. Follow appropriate procedures for storage of eye protective devices. _____

REFERENCES

Contact Lense News Backgrounder. 1979. St. Louis: American Optometric Association.
Eye Protection Devices for Students and Teachers. In *Code of Iowa*, Section 280.20.
Job Safety and Health. 1975. 3 (7):17-21. Washington, D.C.: Occupational Safety and Health Administration.
Practice for occupational and eye-face protection, ANSI-Z87.1-1979. New York: American National Standards Institute.

4 Physical Sciences

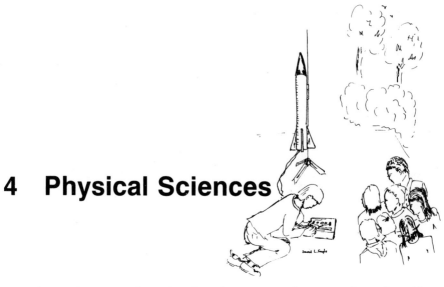

Attention to safety in the elementary classroom is primarily the responsibility of the classroom teacher. As students learn to work with materials related to the physical sciences it is the teacher's responsibility to establish and maintain a safety conscious attitude and mode of behavior.

Much of the equipment used in teaching elementary physical science may be familiar to elementary students. It may even be found in their homes. As a result, students may be careless in handling material and/or try to duplicate activities at home. Thus the classroom teacher must stress safety in choice and use of materials along with appropriate behavior. Knowing the reasons for certain procedures may help students understand the need for safety considerations. The time and thought devoted to safety is invaluable in preventing injuries and possible accidents.

This chapter reviews the possible kinds of injuries relative to the use of physical science equipment, and presents safety hints for typical units of elementary science.

POSSIBLE KINDS OF INJURIES

Physical science equipment, if not properly handled, can cause the following kinds of injuries:

1. *Cuts or punctures*. Students need instruction in the use of such cutting tools as razor blades and knives. Only single-edged razor blades should be used. Cutting should be done on a hard surface with plenty of work space. Sharp cutting edges are actually safer than wornout dull edges. Students should be told to always cut away from themselves.

Glass tubing, containers, and thermometers need to be handled carefully to avoid cuts. Glass jars should be wrapped with electrical tape to prevent glass from shattering if dropped. Hand mirrors should be taped across the back to avoid shattering; it is recommended that metal mirrors be used instead of glass mirrors.

Motorized equipment should have guards over belts and pulleys to reduce the possibility of entanglement of clothing, hair, or hands.

2. *Burns.* Many activities in physical science need a heat source. These sometimes present safety problems. Alcohol burners, candles, and propane burners all have a visible indication of heat, which students should recognize as a danger, and they also have the hazard of easily igniting material.

Electrical hot plates and ovens are not as obvious visual dangers as some other sources of heat. Such heat sources need to be located away from careless contact before, during, or after their use. A "WARNING: HOT" sign might serve as a visible reminder.

Use of a heating source necessitates specific instructions; use of heat-resistant gloves and handling materials; and restrictions on loose clothing and long hair. See Chapter 5, Chemicals and Their Handling, for further information.

3. *Explosions.* Glass materials subject to temperature extremes should be heat resistant to prevent shattering.

Dry-cell batteries need to be handled carefully, since they may explode if heated. Dry cells not designed to be recharged may also explode if placed in a recharger.

Fluids should not be heated in a closed container. Explosions may occur if the expanding steam is not vented.

SAFETY CONSIDERATIONS FOR TYPICAL SCIENCE UNITS

Physical science may be incorporated within a variety of units in an elementary curriculum. The headings below suggest topics involving physical science. Obviously, the specific concepts studied will vary with curriculum design. The hints listed are intended to help teachers keep safety in mind when planning units appropriate for any grade level.

Sound

The study of sound may include activities and experiments related to how sound is produced; how sound travels; and several characteristics of sound, such as pitch, loudness, quality, and resonance.

The major safety consideration of this unit would be the means of sound production. Devices commonly used could present some dangers. Stretched wires and rubber bands might break. Glass containers with or without water at different levels should be tapped gently so the glass doesn't shatter. Good hygiene needs to be considered when a number of students blow in the same instrument or tubing.

The intensity of sound deserves attention. Permanent damage to hearing can be done when students are subjected to sounds that are too loud.

The unit used to measure sound intensity is the *decibel*.

Sounds of 120 decibels and above may damage hearing.

Table 4.1 shows the approximate decibel levels of common sounds and the effects upon humans.

TABLE 4.1. Decibel Levels of Common Sounds

Sound Sources	Decibels	Effect
Jet airplane, takeoff		
at close range	155	
Frequent exposure to rock		Possibly damaging
music at close range	140	to hearing
Thunder	110	
Riveting jackhammer	100	
Automobile horns	95	
Freeway traffic	80	Annoying
Vacuum cleaner	70	
Typing noise	65	
Ordinary speaking voice	60	
Residential street traffic	50	
Average home noises	40-50	Acceptable
Soft music	30	
Whisper	10-20	
Breathing	10	

Matter

The study of matter is really the discovery of "what things are made of." This generally begins with experiences using the five senses. Later, opportunities are provided for understanding physical and chemical changes. In the upper elementary grades scientific phenomena regarding the structure of matter and how changes occur can be demonstrated. The use of scientific processes is most important in developing understanding.

Exploration of the physical environment involves many experiments and experiences that continue beyond classroom boundaries. Teachers must use discrimination in their selection of materials for experiments and investigative procedures.

In the primary grades a study of the five senses is common. Care needs to be taken in selecting substances, especially for smelling and tasting. The teacher must be aware of students who have food allergies. Students should be taught never to taste or smell materials unless the teacher specifically gives permission to do so. Liquids need to be placed in containers that will not spill easily. Containers should be labeled--even if the labels are disguised during closely supervised tasting and smelling experiments.

Experiments with acids, bases, salts, solutions, and mixtures found in elementary science texts are usually carefully tested. Students must be reminded to follow directions exactly and handle the materials safely. Occasionally such dangerous chemicals as drain cleaners and toilet cleaners might be brought into the classroom. These should be kept only in the original containers so their danger is easily recognizable.

The best suggestion for teachers unfamiliar with the chemistry of any substance is: *read labels*. If the teacher is unfamiliar with the chemicals listed an expert should be contacted. See Chapter 5, Chemicals and Their Handling, for further information.

Students should be warned not to experiment--randomly mixing substances they find at home. Household cleaning agents can be potentially dangerous chemicals! Primary children especially need to be warned of dangerous chemicals at home, where accidental poisoning is a real danger. Schools can take an active part in this safety education. By federal law, the third full week in March is designated as National Poison Prevention Week. Teacher resources relevant to this week and year-round poison prevention activities may be ordered from:

> National Planning Council for National Poison Prevention Week
> P.O. Box 1543
> Washington, DC 20013

The Home Safety Checklist is an example of materials available. This accidental poison prevention inventory is a positive means of creating awareness of dangerous household chemicals and its use can provide a service within the community.

Teachers and parents may be interested in the National Poison Center Network. This nationwide network operates twenty-four hours a day, seven days a week to deal with poison emergencies. Poison control centers are listed uner "Poison" in the phone book. The National Poison Center Network has developed "Mr. Yuk" stickers that are readily identified by students. These stickers can be affixed to dangerous substances to lessen the dangers of accidental poisoning.

Heat

The study of heat in the elementary curriculum involves heat production; heat measurement; heat transfer; and heat effects. Primary safety considerations of this unit are the prevention of burns and cuts.

Thermometers used by students in elementary classrooms should be easy to handle and encased in a sturdy holder. Alcohol thermometers, not mercury, are recommended.

Glassware used in experiments with heat should be in good condition and resistant to heating and cooling.

Temperature studies often use a heat source. Electric hot plates are preferred, if available in the quantity needed for classroom use. If heat is needed for small group work, use candles in secure holders. Sterno-type heat sources are appropriate sources for some activities. Alcohol burners are also satisfactory, but if spilled, flammable liquid spreads quickly. Because of the difficulty in adjusting the flame, bunsen and propane burners are safe to use only if under direct teacher supervision.

Heat resistant equipment is necessary for handling hot materials; many different kinds of equipment may be used, such as gloves, tongs, and hot pads. Do not use asbestos materials. Children need specific instructions so they can keep hair and loose

clothing from catching fire. They should be cautioned not to reach
across an open flame.

Matches are a source of much curiosity to children. Students
need to be told why matches are not playthings and instructed also
how to use matches carefully. Such hints as closing a matchbox or
matchbook before striking, and then striking the match away from
the body are simple safety measures. Matches in the classroom must
be under teacher control and put away after every use. See Chapter
10, Fire Protection and Control, for further information.

Light
The study of light in elementary schools is based upon investigations into the behavior of light. Specific activities relate

---

Home Safety Check List

Dear (name of teacher):

I took this checklist home and helped my family check all of
the places where potentially poisonous products might be found.
We talked about safer places and ways to keep things that might be
poisonous. I promised always to ask before tasting anything I
found around the house. I'm going to try to protect other children who live in my home or come to visit us, too, so they will be
safe from poisoning.
Here are the places my family looked to see if potentially
poisonous products were packaged in safety containers and stored
safely, out of reach of small children:

Bathrooms	[]	Dining area	[]	Workshop	[]
Bedrooms	[]	Basement	[]	Utility room	[]
Kitchen	[]	Garage	[]	Special storage places	[]
Living room	[]	Attic	[]	Porch and under the porch	[]
Closets	[]	Yard	[]	Other	[]

My family looked especially for these things:

Kerosene and gasoline	[]	Disinfectants and deodorants	[]
Lye and bleaches	[]	Mothballs and pesticides	[]
Soaps and detergents	[]	Paint remover and turpentine	[]
Polishes and cleaning powders	[]	All kinds of sprays	[]
Ant and rat poison	[]	Fertilizer and weed killers	[]
Aspirin and other medicines (including vitamins)	[]	Toilet bowl cleaners and drain cleaners	[]

Now we hope that our home is poison-proof!

Sincerely yours,

(name of child)

to shadows, reflection, refraction, and use of optical instruments. Urge caution when students are using overhead projectors or slide projectors to cast shadows. The lamps get extremely hot and may cause burns. Regular light bulbs in exposed sockets need to be handled carefully also.

To avoid eye damage students should be cautioned about looking directly into high-intensity lights.

A variety of lenses and prisms may be used in investigating the behavior of light. These need to be handled carefully to prevent shattering. Metal mirrors of polished aluminum are easily handled by children. If glass mirrors are used they should be taped across the back.

Magnifying lenses should have secure handles and be easy for students to use. Many plastic lenses are available and have different degrees of magnification. Students are often fascinated by the heat produced at the focal point of a lens and often try to start fires. The proper use of a magnifying lens needs to be explained.

The study of photography is related to this unit. If students are developing their own pictures, urge caution. Set behavior expectations while using the necessary chemicals. Light-tight-roll-film tanks are recommended for developing the film. Goggles should be worn during the processing.

Few elementary students are likely to have experience with lasers, but if a speaker happens to bring laser equipment into the classroom, safety needs to be a consideration.

Machines

The study of machines involves activities with simple machines, engines, and tools. Simple equipment from kitchens and workshops is useful for experiments. Many toys illustrate basic concepts, too. Safety is still a consideration in any experiences planned.

Small models of the steam engine are potentially dangerous. Extreme caution needs to be used in demonstrating them because vents can become plugged and cause boilers to explode. Wheel- and chain-driven apparatuses need to be treated with special caution.

Allowances for adequate ventilation must be made when demonstrating two- and four-cycle engines. Dangerous levels of carbon monoxide may result if ventilation is limited.

Hand tools used in the classroom need careful consideration. Equipment must not be too large for children to use safely. Students need to be shown how to use tools properly. Adequate work space also must be available. A good rule of thumb to consider is not to use hammers with a weight of more than 10 oz (284 g). Goggles are especially necessary when power equipment is used. Specific instructions and supervision are a part of planning for any project. Elementary teachers may get help from an industrial arts teacher in how to use basic hand tools and power tools.

Cardboard carpentry is an activity used in some school settings. Many pieces of very functional science equipment may be

built. It is very important that the teacher use an approved fire-
proofing procedure on all finished products.

Electricity and Magnetism
      Electricity and magnetism are everywhere in the lives of chil-
dren, and well-planned experiments with them provide outlets for
the natural tendencies of children to investigate.
      Experimenting with magnets is relatively safe. Students need
to be reminded to handle iron filings carefully. They must not
blow on the filings because this might cause filings to lodge in
someone's eyes. Machine shop filings may be used; however, clean-
ness, size, and sharpness should be considered carefully.
      Electrical experiments can be done safely by following direc-
tions and using common sense. Students need to understand and have
respect for electricity rather than be fearful of it.
      Many experiments may require that insulated wire be stripped.
Wire strippers may be used. Students should be taught to strip the
wires using motions directed away from their bodies.
      Experiments should be done using storage batteries or dry
cells as a source of direct current (DC) electricity. You cannot
get a shock directly from a dry cell. Household current, which is
alternating current (AC) electricity, is too dangerous for classroom experiments.
      When using dry-cell batteries students should be cautioned
about leaving batteries connected in a complete circuit. Short
circuits are very damaging to the batteries; they often produce a
great amount of heat and might cause a fire. Students can gain
knowledge of this by a demonstration of a short circuit and feeling
the heat generated. Caution--the wires get hot quickly!
      Dry-cell batteries should not be heated. It could cause them
to explode due to the moisture in the battery. Only batteries that
are rechargeable should be placed in a battery recharger.
      Electrical experiments using chemicals demand some caution.
Some chemicals may not be safe for students to handle and teacher
demonstration may be necessary.
      Lead storage batteries such as automobile batteries contain
sulphuric acid, which is extremely dangerous. Both the strength of
the acid and the ability to produce great quantities of current are
dangers. Students should be told not to experiment with these
powerful and potentially dangerous batteries.
      Direct supervision by the teacher is needed when examining the
inside of an incandescent bulb. The glass is thin and shatters
easily. Do not break a fluorescent bulb. The mercury coating on
the inside of the glass is harmful.
      It would be wise for teachers to give students some general
rules regarding the use of alternating current electricity.

1. Be certain your hands are dry and you are not standing in water
    while touching an electrical appliance or switch.
2. Use only electrical appliances and cords that are in good con-
    dition.

3. Keep electric cords from rubbing against other objects.
4. Do not overload electrical sockets and circuits.
5. Always replace a used fuse with one that will carry the same current (amperage).
6. Be certain the switch on an electrical appliance is off before disconnecting the appliance.
7. Never work on electric wires, connections, or appliances while the wires are plugged into a wall outlet.
8. Make certain that electrical appliances and equipment are grounded and approved by Underwriters' Laboratories or another nationally recognized testing laboratory.

Solar and Nuclear Energy
    Energy education is becoming a more important part of the science curriculum, with many experiments available, especially for solar energy. Care needs to be exercised in handling solar ovens, cookers, and collectors. A large amount of heat is collected in a short period of time; students need to be cautioned to prevent burns.
    Nuclear energy affords few opportunities for experimentation. A Geiger counter might be available for demonstration. Be certain to follow instructions in its use. Radioactive disks should be purchased only from competent dealers. Disposal of such disks *should only be done by such experts* as civil defense personnel and/ or local fire departments.
    Any speakers brought in should keep safety in mind as they explain, demonstrate, and discuss nuclear energy with the students.

Flight
    Flight in inner or outer space is a natural part of the elementary curriculum in this age. Students are very interested in the principles of flight applied to kites, balloons, airplanes, rockets, and satellites. Many activities are available to involve children in active learning.
    Children flying kites need to be in large areas with much open space. They should be reminded to stay away from electrical wires and *always to use cord rather than wire. Never fly kites when rain is falling.* The wet cord can become a good conductor for electricity.
    The study of lighter-than-air flight may involve making large balloons to be filled with hot air. This should be a teacher demonstration because use of a heat source with flammable material is potentially dangerous.
    The release of helium-filled balloons is frequently done in elementary schools. Teachers and students need to recognize that this is not an environmentally sound activity because balloons are not biodegradeable. If balloons are used, notes may be attached asking finders to dispose of them properly.
    Do not let students inhale helium. Asphyxiation can result if students are unable to get enough oxygen into their lungs.
    Paper airplanes are a fun experiment. Set rules so no one is

hit in the eye by the point of an airplane. Gas-powered model air-
planes need to be handled carefully. They have a flammable fuel
and their flight is sometimes difficult to control.

Rocketry is a hobby that interests many students. Launching
the rockets poses some danger, and remote-control launchers are the
safest way to handle this problem. *Do not let students build their
own rocket engines.* Companies producing rocket models list specific safety guidelines: appropriate size of engines to use, safe
construction of rocket models, and directions for launching. *Read
all directions carefully!* Your community may have some guidelines
as to launching sites, so check with local officials if you have
questions. Do not allow students to experiment randomly with the
rocket engines. Supervision is always necessary.

Astronomy
Study of the solar system and universe has few safety problems. However, students must be cautioned not to look directly at
the sun because of possible damage to the eyes. Viewing of the
sun, especially during an eclipse, must be done by viewing an in-
direct image. Pinhole cameras or a simple camera may be used to
project the image.

Viewing the moon or a lunar eclipse directly does not pose a
danger to vision. The use of binoculars for viewing lunar eclipses
can be very interesting.

Weather
Weather instruments can generally be handled quite safely by
students. Use thermometers that are easy to handle and encased in
a sturdy holder. Alcohol-base thermometers are recommended. Be
cautious when using a sling psychrometer to determine relative hu-
midity--allow plenty of space around the user.

During a weather unit children should be warned of the potential danger of lightning during electrical storms. They should be
told where and how to seek safety. Motor vehicles tend to be a
safe source of shelter as are buildings with approved lightning-
arresting systems. Lightning is a serious hazard to be considered
in planning field trips and outdoor activities.

The danger of tornadoes is also a concern, especially in the
Midwest. Most schools have a procedure to follow during a tornado
watch, but it is wise to review this for children periodically. If
your school doesn't have an established procedure, then it is recommended that one be established and practiced.

Geology
The study of rocks and minerals often necessitates a rock
pick (hammer). Students should wear goggles and gloves while chip-
ping away at rocks whether in the classroom or on a field trip.

Homemade or school-made chemical volcanoes are not recommended. The heat necessary for a chemical reaction is often intense
and toxic fumes may result. See Chapter 5, Chemicals and Their
Handling, for further information.

These safety considerations for typical science units are not meant to be all-inclusive. The best means of preventing accidents is to always keep safety in mind when planning student activities. Attentiveness, foreseeing possible safety-related problems, and common sense are necessary.

The classroom teacher sets the tone for science experiences by stressing safety in the choice of activities, by giving proper directions, and by following correct scientific procedures. Students will begin to model their behaviors and attitudes after those of the teacher.

Science investigations are fun and stretch the horizons of the mind. Concern for safety should not prevent teachers from sharing exciting science experiences with their students. Careful planning helps to remove the fear of accidents from the excitement of learning.

CHECKLIST

1. Know the safe procedures to use when students are
   working with:
   Cutting tools   _____
   Glass tubing   _____
   Thermometers   _____
   Mirrors (glass)   _____
   Motorized equipment   _____
2. Know what kind of safe heat sources to use and how
   to use them properly.   _____
3. Be aware of safe instructional procedures for
   teaching the following topics:
   Sound   _____
   Matter   _____
   Heat   _____
   Optics   _____
   Machines   _____
   Electricity/magnetism   _____
   Solar and nuclear energy   _____
   Flight   _____
   Astronomy   _____
   Weather   _____
   Geology   _____

REFERENCES

Dean, Robert A.: Dean, Melanie Messer; and Motz, La Moine L. 1978. *Safety in the elementary classroom.* Prepared by the NSTA Subcommittee on Safety. Washington, D.C.: National Science Teachers Association.
Gerlovich, Jack, and Downs, Gary E. 1981. *Better science through safety.* Ames: Iowa State University Press.

Graf, Rudolf. 1964. *Safe and simple electrical experiments.* New York: Dover Publications.

A guide to teaching poison prevention in kindergarten and primary grades. n.d. Washington, D.C.: U.S. Consumer Product Safety Commission.

North Carolina Department of Public Instruction. 1977. *Safety first in science teaching.* New York: Holt, Rinehart, and Winston.

Reuben, Gabriel. 1960. *Electricity experiments for children.* New York: Dover Publications.

5 Chemicals and Their Handling

CHEMICALS COMMONLY FOUND IN ELEMENTARY SCIENCE CLASSROOMS

Innumerable chemicals may be present in the elementary science classroom, compounds ranging from simple inorganic to complex and from relatively innocuous to hazardous. In older classrooms, it is probable that chemicals are being stored that once were considered safe but now are recognized as hazardous.

The beginning part of this chapter describes materials likely to be found in most elementary science rooms. More toxic substances are discussed in later sections of the chapter.

Acids

The word *acid* is from the Latin word *acidus*, meaning sour; sourness is a common characteristic of acids. Acids occur in both living and nonliving systems. For example, citric acid is found in citrus fruits (living), while sulfuric acid spews forth from Mount St. Helens (nonliving) when it is active. One can determine if a substance is an acid using *litmus* (a vegetable substance derived from lichens). An acid will turn blue litmus paper red (or pink). Acids contain the element hydrogen bonded to another element in such a way that hydrogen ions (H^+) can form in solution. *Strong acids* can produce high concentrations of hydrogen ions; *weak acids* never produce high concentrations of hydrogen ions. Since all concentrated strong acids (like hydrochloric acid or sulfuric acid) can damage the skin and eyes, only the weak acids or very dilute strong acids should be used in the elementary classroom. Vinegar is a reasonable choice.

Bases

Bases usually are bitter and feel slippery (like soap) between the fingers. They will turn red (or pink) litmus blue. Many simple bases can yield hydroxide ions (OH^-) in solution.

The common strong bases are potassium hydroxide, sodium hy-

droxide, and ammonia. The first two are extremely caustic and can
cause severe damage to the eyes and skin, while concentrated ammonia can cause severe bronchial irritation. Diluted household
ammonia is a reasonable choice for the classroom.

Salts
       Salts are generally composed of a metal combined with a non-
metal, as in sodium chloride (table salt). Salts are formed when
acids neutralize bases. The health risk of salts varies from almost harmless to highly toxic. Highly toxic ones that should not
be used in the elementary classroom include (but are not limited
to) salts of lead, arsenic, barium, or cadmium as well as metal
fluorides, cyanides, chromates, and dichromates. Only those designated in modern elementary science manuals (such as table salt
[sodium chloride]) should be kept in inventory.

Flammables
       Flammables are substances that readily catch fire and burn in
air. Please read the sections on the storage and labeling of flammable substances before determining which materials to keep.

Hydrogen Peroxide
       It is safe if the 3 percent solution common at drugstores is
purchased. Stronger concentrations (higher percentages) can damage
the skin and should not be used.

Soil Test and Water Analysis Kits
       Commercial companies produce a number of kits containing a
wide variety of inorganic and organic reagents and dyes. While
most of the chemicals in these kits are relatively harmless, some
do contain potentially harmful materials if care is not exercised.
For instance some kits contain strong bases (like potassium hydroxide); in a few cases, even "cancer suspect" agents (like formaldehyde) may be present. Hundreds of different reagents are present in various kits; this manual cannot describe them all but the
manufacturers are required by law to use warnings on labels if a
hazard exists.
       On most harmless agents a warning appears: "Do not ingest."
"Harmful if swallowed" appears on moderately toxic compounds.
"Fatal if swallowed" appears on highly toxic substances.
       Literature in the kits gives specific directions to be fol-
lowed and also lists precautions for hazardous materials. The
companies are also willing to supply *material safety data sheets*
upon request for any reagent they sell. Such sheets describe hazards, incompatibility, handling, storage, disposal, spillage, and
first aid for each reagent.

CHEMICAL STORAGE
       Every chemical used in the classroom should have a definite
storage place and should be returned to that location after use.
This will provide security against unauthorized access and protect

the reagents from contamination, heat, and other factors. Ideally, chemicals should be stored away from the classroom. If, however, they must be stored in the classroom, separate, lockable cabinets would be desirable.

Acids and Bases

It would be wise to store acids away from bases. If a store-room with open shelves is being used, store the acids and bases on separate shelves. Strong acids can react with strong bases rather violently and produce heat and spattering; avoid that possibility with proper storage.

Flammable Liquids and Solvents

Many fires in schools are caused by improper storage and han-dling of flammable liquids; avoid keeping any in the classroom if possible. Common examples of those to avoid would be gasoline, kerosene, benzene, acetone, toluene, mineral spirits, lacquer thin-ner, or turpentine. Materials suggested for use by common science manuals (motor oil or transmission fluid) pose much less risk, but still should not be handled near an open flame.

Methyl alcohol (also called methanol or wood alcohol) is one of the commonest highly flammable liquids kept in schools. It is used in alcohol burners and is the major component of ditto fluids for spirit duplicating machines. Materials of this flammability should be stored in metal containers and in suitably designed cab-inets. (The largest glass container that the National Fire Protec-tion Association [NFPA] allows for this class of liquid is a one pint [500 ml] bottle.) Store only the quantities necessary to carry out current activities in the classroom. If large quantities (several gallons) of flammables need to be stored, ask the science supervisor, principal, or building custodian to find a suitable lo-cation away from classrooms.

If you must store gallon (liter) quantities of flammable liq-uids in the classroom, the best choice is an Occupational Safety and Health Administration (OSHA) listed or Underwriters' Labora-tories (UL) approved safety container. These resist damage, won't break, permit convenient pouring and easy carrying. They come in a variety of sizes from one pint (500 ml) to several gallons (liters). They are made from various materials, including steel and high den-sity polyethylene, and they are available from safety supply com-panies. They have spring-loaded caps that close automatically and are designed to prevent a spark from "flashing back" into the con-tainer. They also will vent vapors without rupturing if the room gets hot.

If for any reason gasoline must be on the premise, it should be kept in a container specifically approved by the state for such storage. If doubts exist as to the proper container for the in-tended purpose, ask the local fire marshal.

Here are some final do's and don'ts on flammable storage:

1. Storage areas should be cool (between 55°F [18°C] and 80°F [27°C]), dry, and well ventilated. (Consider the temperature

during summer vacations. Does the sun ever shine directly on
the flammables or even on their storage cabinet?)
2. Don't expose flammables to a source of ignition--candle, alcohol burner, or a burning match.
3. Store paints and aerosols with other flammables.
4. Don't store any flammable material in a standard household refrigerator. Exposed electrical connections can provide the ignition source to cause an explosion.

Materials Not Recommended for Usage in the Classroom
      *Halogenated hydrocarbons (carbon tetrachloride), formaldehyde,
mercury and its salts, alkali metals (sodium and potassium), caustic alkalies (potassium hydroxide and sodium hydroxide), pesticides, cyanides, and unlabeled containers should not be present in
the classroom. The following section on toxicity will elaborate.*

TOXICITY
      The word *toxicity* refers to those materials that cause damage
to humans. Whether or not a substance is toxic is highly dependent
on quantity. For instance, fluorides are clearly recognized as
poisons even in relatively low concentrations, yet, at about one
part per million, fluoride has very beneficial effects in preventing tooth decay and is thus deliberately added to many drinking
water supplies.
      The four routes of entry of toxic substances into the body
are: inhalation, ingestion, absorption through the skin or eyes,
or injection. Ingestion is the most common cause of harm in children. Since most poisonings take place during usage, children
should not be left unattended in the classroom with chemicals present, and as many hazardous compounds should be eliminated from the
inventory as possible.

Inhalation
      Of the routes by which toxic chemicals can enter the body, in-
halation is the most dangerous and most rapid acting (Muir 1977).
It produces poisoning by absorption through the mucous membrane of
the mouth, throat, and nose. Be sure to keep lids on any containers of volatile liquids; work with small quantities; provide adequate ventilation. *First aid*: The essential treatment is to remove the person to fresh air. For minor symptoms, little else
needs to be done but to maintain surveillance during recovery; for
a more serious reaction, seek medical attention. Always document
any personal injury problems! Report all such injuries to the
school nurse and/or school administrator.

Ingestion
      Many chemicals in the classroom are extremely dangerous if
they enter the mouth and are swallowed. During experiments allow
no food or drink in the room that could lead to accidental ingestion of chemicals. Chemical tasting by students should be done
only under direct teacher supervision! *First aid*: Encourage the

victim to drink large amounts of water while enroute to medical assistance. Attempt to learn exactly what was ingested. Do not attempt to induce vomiting without a physician's advice.

Absorption

The main portals of entry through the skin are the hair follicles, sebaceous glands, sweat glands, and cuts and abrasions of the outer layer of skin (*Prudent practices* 1981). Methyl alcohol is a very common chemical that is absorbed through the skin; many types of pesticides are also. *First aid for skin contact*: Immediately flush with cold water for several minutes. Wash by using soap or a mild detergent with water. If a visible burn appears, seek medical attention. *First aid for eye contact*: Flush with water for 15 minutes, holding eyelids apart if necessary. (Use a gentle stream of water.) Seek medical attention whether or not symptoms of damage appear, and provide information on chemicals involved.

Injection

Exposure to chemicals by injection is unlikely, but it can occur by mechanical injury from broken glass contaminated with a chemical.

The poison control center's toll-free number in Iowa is 1-800-272-6477; *call for additional advice at any time.*

SPECIFIC CHEMICALS TO AVOID

A number of substances have no place in the elementary classroom. The following list describes materials that were once common, but are now known to pose risks greater than the value of storing or handling them.

Mercury and Mercury Compounds

They can be absorbed into the body by inhalation, ingestion, or contact with skin. Mercury is a subtle poison, the effects of which are cumulative and not readily reversible (Muir 1977,52). Continued exposure to small concentrations of vapor may result in severe nervous disturbances, including tremor of the hands, insomnia, loss of memory, instability, and depression. If one insists on the use of mercury, it should be by teacher demonstration and only in a well-ventilated room and over a spillage tray.

Alkali Metals

The alkali metals most often used in secondary chemistry labs (but sometimes borrowed for demonstrations by elementary teachers) are lithium, sodium, and potassium. They react vigorously with many substances, including water. When they react with water they form very strong bases and liberate hydrogen, a flammable gas. The heat of reaction can ignite the hydrogen.

Caustic Alkalies

The caustic alkalies most frequently found in labs are potas-

sium hydroxide and sodium hydroxide. They can produce permanent,
irreversible eye injury in less than a minute; destruction of the
cornea begins within seconds after contact. They often damage the
eyes more than strong acids do.

Carbon Tetrachloride
        This compound was once commonly used for insect killing jars
and also in fire extinguishers. Toxicology books today list the
following warnings:

1. Avoid breathing vapor.
2. Avoid contact with skin and eyes.
3. Inhalation of high concentrations of vapor can cause headaches,
    mental confusion, depression, fatigue, loss of appetite, nau-
    sea, vomiting, and coma.
4. Ingestion is even worse; swallowing as little as one teaspoon
    of carbon tetrachloride can be fatal. Many deaths have oc-
    curred from accidental ingestion.

Chloroform
        Inhalation exposure to chloroform can produce dizziness, nau-
sea, and headache; high exposure can cause liver and kidney damage.
Liquid chloroform in the eye will produce corneal damage.

Methylenedichloride (also called methylene chloride)
        This compound is sometimes recommended as a "safe" substitute
for carbon tetrachloride in insect killing jars. Muir (1977,222)
lists the following warnings:

1. Avoid breathing vapor.
2. Avoid contact with skin and eyes.
3. The vapor irritates the eyes and respiratory system and may
    cause headaches and nausea.
4. Assumed to be poisonous if taken by mouth.

Other Halogenated Hydrocarbons
        This class of compounds (which includes the three compounds
listed above) is made up of organic substances containing chlorine,
bromine, or fluorine. Many of these substances present health
risks by their presence in the elementary classroom.

Formaldehyde (formalin is a 30-55 percent aqueous solution of
formaldehyde)
        Formaldehyde is used in preserving biological specimens. In-
gestion of 3 oz (100 ml) is almost certainly fatal within 48 hours.
Inhalation of vapors may result in severe irritation and edema of
the upper respiratory tract, burning and stinging of the eyes, and
headache. Formaldehyde is now on the OSHA list of suspected carcinogens. (Purchase commercially prepared preservatives that contain no formaldehyde if specimen collecting is done.)

Pesticides

Nearly all pesticides can either cause skin damage or be absorbed through the skin or both. One of the more toxic subgroups, the organophosphorous insecticides, can be absorbed by inhalation, ingestion, or topical contact and can cause damage to the nervous system. Keep all pesticides out of the classroom and restrict their handling to the instructor if plant growing projects require their use.

Arsenic

Inorganic arsenic is now on the OSHA carcinogen list.

Cyanides

These are highly toxic and produce deadly hydrogen cyanide gas if they come in contact with acids.

Indicator Powders

Teacher use only!

Unlabeled Bottles

Hazard! Disposal mandatory!

GENERAL RECOMMENDATIONS

1. Do not allow eating or drinking during any experiment where chemicals are being used.
2. Do not allow students to mix chemicals without direction. Do only experiments authorized and supervised by the teacher. Allow no horseplay!
3. Think, act, and encourage safety until it becomes a habit for all.
4. Do not allow students to touch or taste chemicals unless directed to do so.
5. Store all chemicals in a secure place.
6. Maintain only small quantities of needed chemicals in the classroom.
7. Dispose of any substance that is not properly labeled according to approved local, state, or federal guidelines.
8. Dispose of any chemical that has been kept beyond its shelf life according to approved local, state, or federal guidelines. Look for corroded caps, leaking containers, and discoloration.
9. Inspect the classroom periodically for potential hazards. Report findings to the science supervisor or building administrator. Follow up if necessary.
10. Do not allow students to point the open end of a test tube being heated at themselves or anyone else.
11. Do not allow students to return unused chemicals to stock bottles.
12. Have appropriate waste receptacles available for disposal of matches and other waste. The sink is not acceptable.

13. Do not do any experiment using flames or other sources of ignition near stored flammable liquids, and do not heat flammable liquids.
14. Do not allow storage of flammable liquids in a standard refrigerator.
15. Do not allow food to be kept in any refrigerator containing chemicals.
16. If (against this author's advice) strong acids or bases are being handled, appropriate eye protection should be worn. (Eye protection may be necessary even for such operations as cutting brittle wire.)
17. If substances known to penetrate the skin (for example, methanol) are being handled (by the instructor), protective gloves should be worn.
18. Wipe up chemical spills at once.
19. If acids or bases are spilled on clothing, students should notify the instructor at once.
20. If acids or bases are spilled on skin or eyes, immediately flush with water for several minutes. Do not attempt to neutralize acid or base spills on the skin or eyes. In the case of eye contact, seek medical attention whether damage is evident or not.
21. Always work in well-ventilated areas.
22. Avoid:
    a) volcano demonstrations using ammonium dichromate
    b) demonstrations of dust explosions or flash explosions or carburetors
    c) making soap using lye (sodium hydroxide)
    d) sublimation of potassium permanganate
    e) any experiment using carbon tetrachloride, benzene, chloroform, or mercury
    f) use of radioactive materials
    g) demonstration of flammability of hydrogen gas
    h) use of sulfuric acid in electroplating demonstrations (use sodium sulfate instead)

LABELING

Purchasing Philosophy

The achievement of safe handling, use, and disposal of chemicals begins with the person who requisitions such substances and with the person who approves the purchase order. These personnel must have a concept of what is generally considered safe for elementary school science. Fortunately, some of the newer chemical supply catalogs enumerate hazards for each chemical listed and also make storage and disposal recommendations (*Chemical catalog reference manual* 1981).

Order small quantities of chemicals that will not sit on the shelves for several years. Don't accept any chemical that is not labeled. For chemicals purchased from bona fide science supply houses, insist that the labels correspond to the ANSI-Z129.1 standard, which requires, at a minimum, the following:

a) identification of contents of the container
b) summary of any hazards
c) precautionary information
d) first aid in case of exposure
e) spill and cleanup procedures
f) special instructions to physicians, if appropriate

Since proper labeling of chemicals is fundamental to safe and successful science experiments, students should be taught the importance of adequate identification. Teach them to read labels thoroughly, noting precautions as well as contents.

Making some labels in the classroom can be educational. Be sure to use durable labels that won't fall off and use indelible ink that won't run, even if chemicals contact it. *Remember, any substance that is not properly labeled should be disposed of immediately according to local, state, or federal guidelines.*

The NFPA 704 System
A relatively new system of labeling using a "hazard diagram" is being recommended by the National Fire Protection Association (NFPA). The diagram (see Figure 5.1) is divided into four color-coded segments; the top segment (red) is for indicating flammability; the left segment (blue) is for indicating the health hazard; the right segment (yellow) is for indicating reactivity; the bottom segment (white) is used to identify any special characteris-

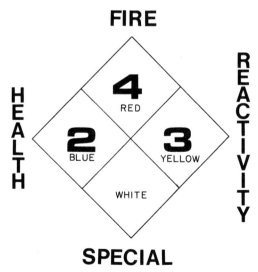

FIG. 5.1. National Fire Protection Association Hazard Coding System.

tics, but will often be blank for chemicals discussed here. A number ranging from 0 to 4 is used in each colored box to indicate the degree of hazard, with 0 being no hazard and 4 signifying an extreme hazard (see Figure 5.2). This has significant advantages over past systems that use more vague statements such as "flammable" or "avoid skin contact."

The hazard diagram for sodium hydroxide (lye) used in making soap serves as an example for discussion and further explanation. The "0" for flammability indicates that no fire hazard exists. The reactivity of "1" indicates that it is normally stable but that under some conditions it is reactive. The "3" for health indicates a strong note of caution; this is a material that, on short exposure, could cause serious injury, even if prompt medical attention were given. (In fact, lye is known to be a severe eye hazard; solid or concentrated solutions destroy tissue on contact.)

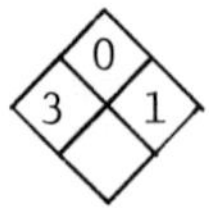

Vegetable oil, on the other hand, bears a hazard diagram that indicates no hazard in health or reactivity and no flammability hazard unless heated.

A sampling of other compounds found in elementary science classrooms is shown below with the respective hazard diagrams (*Standard system* 1980):

corn oil

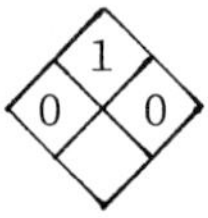

naphthalene or mothballs

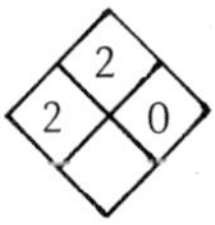

methanol or methyl alcohol or wood alcohol

ethanol or ethyl alcohol or grain alcohol

isopropyl alcohol or rubbing alcohol

carbon tetrachloride

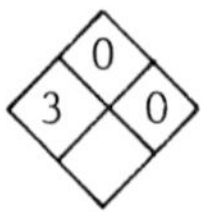

ethylene glycol or antifreeze

gasoline

turpentine

mineral oil

glycerol or glycerine

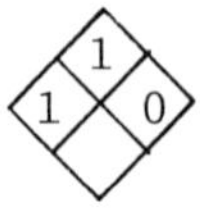

sodium

Identification of Health Hazard Color Code: BLUE		Identification of Flammability Color Code: RED		Identification of Reactivity (Stability) Color Code: YELLOW	
Type of Possible Injury		Susceptibility of Materials to Burning		Susceptibility to Release of Energy	
Signal		Signal		Signal	
4	Materials which on very short exposure could cause death or major residual injury even though prompt medical treatment were given.	4	Materials which will rapidly or completely vaporize at atmospheric pressure and normal ambient temperature, or which are readily dispersed in air and which will burn readily.	4	Materials which in themselves are readily capable of detonation or of explosive decomposition or reaction at normal temperatures and pressures.
3	Materials which on short exposure could cause serious temporary or residual injury even though prompt medical treatment were given.	3	Liquids and solids that can be ignited under almost all ambient temperature conditions.	3	Materials which in themselves are capable of detonation or explosive reaction but require a strong initiating source or which must be heated under confinement before initiation or which react explosively with water.
2	Materials which on intense or continued exposure could cause temporary incapacitation or possible residual injury unless prompt medical treatment is given.	2	Materials that must be moderately heated or exposed to relatively high ambient temperatures before ignition can occur.	2	Materials which in themselves are normally unstable and readily undergo violent chemical change but do not detonate. Also materials which may react violently with water or which may form potentially explosive mixtures with water.
1	Materials which on exposure would cause irritation but only minor residual injury even if no treatment is given.	1	Materials that must be preheated before ignition can occur.	1	Materials which in themselves are normally stable, but which can become unstable at elevated temperatures and pressures or which may react with water with some release of energy but not violently.
0	Materials which on exposure under fire conditions would offer no hazard beyond that of ordinary combustible material.	0	Materials that will not burn.	0	Materials which in themselves are normally stable, even under fire exposure conditions, and which are not reactive with water.

FIG. 5.2. Identifications of Color Codes. (Reproduced with permission from *Standard system for the identification of the fire hazards of materials*, NFPA 704. Copyright 1980, National Fire Protection Association, Quincy, Mass. This reprinted material is not the complete and official position of the NFPA on the referenced subject, which is represented only by the standard in its entirety.)

methylenedichloride or dichloromethane — (1 / 2, 0)

calcium hypochlorite or bleaching powder — (0 / 1, 2 / oxy)

strontium nitrate — (0 / 0, 0)

magnesium nitrate — (0 / 0, 0 / oxy)

sulfuric acid — (0 / 3, 2 / W)

hydrochloric acid — (0 / 3, 0)

The "oxy" in the bottom portion of some of the diagrams indicates that the chemicals are strong oxidizing agents that may ignite combustible materials they contact. The symbol "W" indicates that the compound (for example, sulfuric acid) reacts with water. Many other common classroom chemicals, such as sodium chloride (table salt), pose such low risks that they would rate "0" in all categories.

It is recommended that no student be allowed to handle compounds with a hazard label showing a 2, 3, or 4 in any category. The teacher should, in fact, eliminate from inventory as many compounds as possible with hazard ratings of 2 or above; use the remaining ones for demonstration only.

One of the obvious advantages of the NFPA labeling system is the speed with which one can recognize a potentially hazardous chemical. Consider teaching the students the basics of the system; it has merit in its own right and will, in all probability, become more universally accepted in the future. NFPA ratings for other compounds can be found in a number of reference books and the labels themselves can be purchased commercially in a variety of sizes from safety supply companies.

CHEMICAL SPILLS

Spill control is a universal problem in laboratories; it is safe to assume that any chemical that is handled will eventually be spilled. Be prepared to minimize health and/or fire hazards immediately; that means having the appropriate supplies on hand to deal with spills. The minimum cleanup supplies for the classroom should include paper towels, sponges, broom, dust pan, plastic garbage liners, and sodium bicarbonate. *If a spill occurs*, follow these priorities (*Prudent practices* 1981, 234-35):

a) attend to any person whose skin or clothing may have been affected
b) notify others in the room to stay clear of the spill

c) avoid breathing the vapor if it is a liquid spill
d) remove ignition and heat sources if it is a flammable spill
   then,
e) clean up the spill

Handling Solid Spills
    Since only low toxicity solids belong in the elementary class-
room, the spill can be cleaned up with a broom and dust pan. Place
the material in a solid waste container. (Don't dump solids directly into a metal waste can; place them in a plastic bag first.)

Handling Liquid Spills
    Since only very small quantities of liquids should be stored
or handled in the classroom, it is assumed that spills will be
small also. (Larger spills call for special supplies.)

1. Wear rubber gloves.
2. Absorb the spill with paper towels or a sponge. (*Note*: Don't
    use paper towels to absorb concentrated sulfuric acid.)
3. If the spill is acidic, it can first be neutralized with baking
    soda.
4. If a flammable liquid spill is absorbed with paper towels, re-
    move the towels from the room immediately to avoid a fire haz-
    ard. Take them to a well-ventilated area away from ignition
    sources, preferably outside the building.
5. Carefully clean any splashed liquid from other bottles or ap-
    paratus.
6. If larger acid or base spills are possible, consider keeping a
    bucket of sand/soda ash mixture (commercially available) in the
    room.
7. If larger flammable liquid spills are possible, consider keep-
    ing a bag of vermiculite in the room; as with paper towels, do
    not keep vermiculite soaked with flammable liquid in the class-
    room.

CHEMICAL DISPOSAL
    Disposal of chemicals is a necessary task in all science labs.
It is used not only for eliminating waste after an experiment has
been performed, but also for the following common reasons:

1. Materials have aged and become useless for the intended pur-
    pose.
2. Compound may have lost its label and thus its identity.
3. Safer substitute has been found or an experiment has been per-
    manently abandoned.

    If care is exercised initially in purchasing small quantities
of nontoxic chemicals, then most materials can be flushed down the
sink with large quantities of water. Water-soluble substances are
the most appropriate for this method. If acids and bases are being

dumped, be sure to run plenty of water during disposal. Solutions
of flammable liquids must be sufficiently diluted so they do not
pose a fire hazard.

Remember that the chemicals that are flushed down the drain
and into the sewers go to treatment plants. State and municipal
codes regulate the discharge of wastes in order to avoid pollutants
that would interfere with the performance or operation of publicly
owned treatment plants. If difficult waste disposal problems arise
(for example, mercury), check with officials as to appropriate
action. In Iowa, call the Department of Environmental Quality,
(515) 281-8690, a member of the Iowa Chemical Safety Cadre, (515)
281-3249, or the chemistry department of a local college.

CHECKLIST

1. Have a working knowledge of the following chemicals:
   Acids   _____
   Bases   _____
   Salts   _____
   Flammables   _____
   Hydrogen peroxide   _____
   Others to be used in science activities   _____
2. Use proper procedures for storage of chemicals.   _____
3. Know which materials should not be present in
   the classroom.   _____
4. Have a working knowledge of the NFPA "hazard
   diagram" used for labeling.   _____
5. Know what procedures to follow if a chemical
   spill should occur.   _____
6. Use the proper chemical disposal procedures.   _____
7. Know the ground rules for laboratory procedures
   and student behavior.   _____

REFERENCES

Chemical catalog reference manual. 1981. Batavia, Ill.: Flinn
    Scientific Company.
Gerlovich, Jack A., and Downs, Gary E. 1981. *Better science
    through safety.* Ames: Iowa State University Press.
Green, Michael E., and Turk, Amos. 1978. *Safety in working with
    chemicals.* New York: Macmillan.
Manufacturing Chemists Association. 1972. *Guide for safety in the
    chemical laboratory,* 2d ed. New York: Van Nostrand Reinhold.
Muir, G. D., ed. 1977. *Hazards in the chemical laboratory,* 2d ed.
    London: The Chemical Society.
North Carolina Department of Public Instruction. 1977. *Safety
    first in science teaching.* New York: Holt, Rinehart, and
    Winston.

Prudent practices for handling hazardous chemicals in laboratories. 1981. Washington, D.C.: National Academy Press.

Safety in academic chemistry laboratories, 3d ed. 1979. Washington, D.C.: American Chemical Society.

Standard system for the identification of the fire hazards of materials, NFPA 704. 1980. Boston: National Fire Protection Association.

U.S. Department of Health, Education and Welfare. 1977. *Safety in the school science laboratory.* Cincinnati, Ohio: National Institute for Occupational Safety and Health.

6 Life Sciences

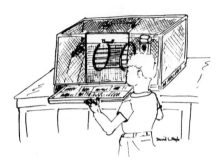

GENERAL SAFETY IDEAS

Life science is a basic subject that all elementary students should study, and the safety and health of the children should be a concern to everyone involved with the elementary schools. Elementary science teachers must practice and teach safety rules and emergency procedures to the students and still allow these students to experience investigations involving life science materials.

When using biological materials the teacher and all participants must always use caution. The teacher must know what live materials are being used in the classroom and what procedures are being used with them. Since it is difficult, if not impossible, to determine in advance what will happen when life science materials are being used, it is advisable to specify safety procedures to be followed by everyone who works or studies in an elementary classroom where live materials will be used.

The teacher should eliminate hazards if possible and then help children learn and understand that they will be expected to use all life science materials with caution and behave sensibly around live matter. The safety rules that apply to the use of living things in the classroom must be consistent with local elementary school safety policies, must have administrative clearance and support, and should fit national professional standards for the housing and care of living things in the classroom. Suggested standards for the storage and handling of preserved biological items should be observed (*Guiding principles* 1969). Wise teachers can get children to help formulate rule interpretations that will help them learn safely.

These suggestions are made because children change developmentally and appropriate life science activities should be designed for the age and capabilities of the children being taught. Rules should be flexible so that students can learn what is sensible and responsible. A teacher who is alert for potential problems will reject activities that are too complex for a given student group.

A relaxed preparedness is a good posture for all elementary science teachers. Professional guidelines have been prepared for handling plants, microorganisms, and animals in the classrooms and these should be followed carefully (*Science safety* 1976). The teacher should have emergency plans for foreseeable sets of circumstances that may occur involving living materials in the classroom.

Appropriate first aid procedures should be a part of the background training of the teacher of elementary science and practice of these procedures should be frequent. If live materials are used in the classroom, the teacher should use an attitude of calmness and flexibility tempered with firmness and reasonableness. Accidents with live materials can be prevented.

It is a wise procedure to explain the behavior expected of elementary students when they work with life science materials. Before starting the learning activities the teacher should explain specific safety practices to be used with live materials. The teacher can also use posters and bulletin boards to emphasize these same safety practices. The posters should include the telephone numbers of the fire department, the police, and an available rescue service.

HAZARDS AND PRECAUTIONS

Because most elementary schools are holistic in their approach to education, it is not expected that an entire classroom will be devoted to science only, let alone life science only. Because of multiple room use in the elementary school, some unique hazards for which precautions must be taken do exist.

Glass or plastic aquaria, terraria, or other organism culture containers should be checked for breaks, cracks, or chips, and students should be advised about care in working with these items. Metal cages and containers need to be examined and kept in good repair. With proper and careful handling, breakable science containment facilities can and should be used safely in life science studies.

All tools and equipment that will be used with live materials should be inspected, and sharp cutting edges should be covered for protection of the user. Sharp objects such as scissors and needles must be used with extra caution. Goggles should be provided if there is the slightest possibility of eye damage during an activity (see Chapter 3, Eye Protection and Eye Care).

Chemicals such as cleaning supplies, household items, fertilizers, preservatives, insecticides, pesticides, and herbicides need to be kept out of reach of the elementary science student. These items should be kept in an adult-access-only storage area that can be locked. The teacher can dispense such items as stains, nontoxic compounds, and preservatives, with special directions about the safe use of the materials.

Two forms of specimens appear in the elementary science classroom. Live materials should be cared for under one of the guidelines related to the care of animals in the class as prepared by one of the professional science organizations (Grafton 1979). This means having only certified healthy laboratory creatures in clean, well-attended containment areas or structures. Preserved specimens should always come from certified laboratory supply companies. The teacher should become familiar with the preservative used on the specimens and possible dangers to students in the presence of these compounds.

If life science materials are used in the elementary class-room, a disposal problem of contaminated litter and spent specimens will exist. Both these items will need to be disposed of following local restrictions on incineration and permission for dumping. (Plastic bags with closures may be very helpful for disposing of such wastes.) All life science areas will need constant attention and will need to be closed down or have special service provided when school is not in session. Good hygiene habits will need to be emphasized with the elementary students in cleaning up after life science materials have been used.

SMALL LIVING THINGS

Most elementary science programs have units that address protists, microbes, and molds. Students need to study and investi-gate these small organisms in learning about biological processes. Students should be taught that there are safe procedures for study-ing these small organisms. Small creatures should not be handled directly but generally in or on culture media in closed vials, capped test tubes, or petri dishes. When studying small organisms the students should not eat or drink, nor should they put their hands near their mouths, noses, or eyes. It is very important that elementary students carefully wash their hands with soap and water after handling small-organism containers. Elementary teachers should decontaminate and discard the spent cultures, using standard procedures such as incineration or other approved disposal tech-niques. The safe study of small things will broaden student aware-ness of the microworld, provide an acceptance of the importance of microorganisms, and encourage caution in future encounters with microbes.

Typically, some students are allergic to mold spores so teach-ers should be careful in their selection of cultures.

ANIMALS

Units on pets often occur in kindergarten curriculums, and animal studies in the elementary classroom are very common. All classroom animals should be from a reputable science supply house. Wild animals should not be brought into the elementary classroom, nor should household pets unless approval has been given by a vet-erinarian and it is accepted school policy. These limitations are required since wild animals or pets can transmit some human dis-eases (such as rabies) from mammals; psittacosis from birds; and salmonellosis from reptiles. If pets are brought to the elementary classroom, they should be handled only by the owners, with others in the class acting as observers. The teacher should teach caution, not fear of animals. If animals are procured for classroom study, be sure they are healthy, free from disease, and nonpoisonous. Careful standards regarding housing, feeding, watering, and cleaning must be met. Classroom animals require much care. Leather gloves should be used when handling live animals to prevent or reduce the opportunity for animal bites, and thus decrease or eliminate one of the commonest science classroom incidents requiring first aid. If a classroom animal does bite or scratch a student, be sure to notify the principal, the school nurse, and the parent. Wash the affected area with soap and water, contact the nurse, notify a local veterinarian, and quarantine the animal for two weeks of observation. If the animal dies, have it examined by the appropriate health authorities.

All the animals useful in the elementary classroom need not be mammals; insects of many types are very interesting to study and many other organisms also can be studied safely. Care needs to be used when studying stinging insects. Some students have a hypersensitivity to either insect stings or insect "bites." Such students need to be identified and special first aid treatment plans need to be made in consultation with the child's family and physician. Live animals that are generally safe and useful in elementary science and are available from biological supply houses include: earthworms, land snails, hermit crabs, sow bugs, crayfish, mealworms, crickets, ants, praying mantises, moths, butterflies, tropical fish, salamanders, tadpoles, xenopus frogs, false chameleons, guinea pigs, and some types of water organisms (hydra, daphnia, planaria). Live animals that are not recommended for student handling are mosquitos, honey bees, tarantulas, turtles, poisonous snakes, parakeets, and skunks. Some of these animals carry human diseases while others have dangerous stings or bites.

Some elementary teachers will elect to use preserved animal specimens with their students. It is wise to procure such preserved material from certified suppliers. Specimens should not be obtained from road kills or from dead animals, because the danger of contamination and disease is too great in such specimens. Fresh specimens should not be used unless they meet all federal and state regulations regarding such material; generally, permits are required to obtain fresh biological materials from slaughterhouses. Teachers should know what chemicals have been used in the preservation of specimens in order to protect students who may have allergies to these chemicals. Supply companies have made advancements in specimen preservatives and are very willing to provide information about the composition of their preservatives. It is suggested that when elementary students dissect preserved specimens, goggles be worn to protect their eyes from preservative splashes. Students, especially those who have known skin allergies to chemicals, should wear gloves during dissections. All preservative spills should be cleaned up by the elementary science teacher. In the chapter "Safety in Biology Settings" in *Better science through*

safety, the authors suggest that special precautions are necessary
in dissection activities: (1) the specimens should be thoroughly
washed before use, (2) the dissecting tools should be in good condition and sharp, (3) the students should work and not play while
dissecting, and (4) the specimens should be carefully stored in
special containers or bags, or refrigerated if they are to be used
again. The spent specimens will need to be disposed of by the elementary science teacher in cooperation with the custodian, with
incineration or burial the preferred methods. Students need to
wash their hands very carefully after all work with preserved animals. Any and all cuts and scratches received should be washed
with soap and water and the student referred to the school nurse.
      Some elementary teachers prefer to have students make collec-
tions of animals. However, since collections require the killing
of specimens, this is a controversial issue. Killing jars are just
that and must be respected for what they are. A good killing jar
for elementary students can be made by using a wide-mouthed jar
completely wrapped with tape to prevent breakage, with a secure,
screw-type lid, and containing a piece of facial tissue or cotton
sprinkled with ethyl acetate in the bottom. Students should use
these killing jars with caution and only when they are getting
specimens for collections of insects, spiders, ticks, mites, centi-
pedes, and millipedes. Ecologists and environmentalists feel it is
best to "look and leave" creatures where they are so that nature's
balance is undisturbed. The procedure of observation only is by
far the safest approach to studying live animals at the elementary
level.

PLANTS
      Plants are vital components of the environment. Every elemen-
tary science program directs students to study plants. Since green
plants capture sunlight through photosynthesis and release free
oxygen into the environment, it is important that plants be a topic
of elementary science. Most plants are safe and helpful to everyone but a few plants pose hazards to children. Elementary students
need to know about dangers from plant irritants and poisons. Table
6.1 provides basic information about a few common dangerous plants.
      Care has been taken to mention only plants that might be
brought to the elementary science classroom. In general, if these
plants are eaten, they may cause some of the following: mouth and
throat irritations, stomach pain, nausea, vomiting, diarrhea, nervous symptoms, irregular heartbeat, breathing difficulties, allergic
responses, convulsions, coma, or death. A few of the plants cause
skin irritations, rashes, blisters, or intense itching. Professional help from a poison center will be needed to counteract the
symptoms caused by these toxic plants. Additional plant problems
are related to special plant structures: thorns, spines, slivers,
stickers, needles, gums, and resins. These items, or by-products
of these items, such as smoke or extracts, can cause children great
difficulties from eye, skin, or lung irritations, puncture wounds,

or infections. First aid should be applied as soon as possible
after students encounter these plants or plant products.
    There are safe ways for elementary students to study all
plants. Plants that have been sealed in plastic bags, sealed as
herbarium mounts, or embedded in plastic can all be handled by students safely. Many useful resources are available for elementary
teachers to use with their students. One such book includes maps,
a glossary, and illustrations, in addition to well-written resumes
(Limburg 1976). If normally safe plants housed in the elementary
classroom or parts of these plants have been determined to cause
allergic responses in a student or students, these plants should be
removed from the classroom.
    Some related problems of keeping plants in the elementary
science classroom include the use of various toxic substances. If
the plants require fertilizer in order to grow, the compounds in
the fertilizer may be dangerous to students. If the plants are
treated with fungicides or pesticides to control infestations or if
plant herbicides are used for some reason, all of the compounds may
be toxic to students; therefore the teacher must exercise caution
in using these substances or mixtures. The proper use of hazardous
chemicals can be taught in this plant unit. When students work directly with plants and use tools in caring for plants, there are
opportunities for cuts, scrapes, and abrasions. General first aid
procedures should be used in treating these conditions.

TABLE 6.1. Selected Dangerous Plants

Plant Type	Leaves	Stems	Roots	Flowers	Fruits or seeds	Pollen	Spores
Cherry tree	X	X					
Poison ivy	X	X	X	X	X		
Potato	X	X					
Tomato	X	X					
Rhubarb	X						
Nightshade	X	X	X	X	X		
Poinsettia	X						
Hydrangea	X	X					
Dieffenbachia	X	X	X	X			
Foxglove	X			X		X	
Philodendron	X	X	X	X			
Oak tree	X				X		
Mistletoe					X		
Mushrooms (certain)		X					X
English ivy	X				X		
Bittersweet	X		X		X		
Molds							X
Santana	X	X	X	X	X		
Oleander	X	X			X		
Yew tree					X		
Castor beans	X				X	X	
Ragweed				X	X		
Lily of the valley	X						
Iris			X				
Jack-in-the-pulpit	X	X	X	X	X		
Daffodils			X				

It is advisable that elementary life science teachers use recommended safety practices at all times with all activities involving elementary students. There are safe ways to study microscopic creatures, animals, and plants. If students have the misfortune of having an accident after the best safety procedures have been used, then the teacher in charge must use "appropriate" emergency procedures. Elementary students need to be exposed to life science materials in a dynamic science setting where good positive safety procedures are practiced at all times.

CHECKLIST

1. Inspect all equipment and supplies that will be used with life science materials to verify that they are safe for use by elementary students.   _____
2. Procure all life science materials from reliable supply firms that verify the safety of their products for elementary science students.   _____
3. Be sure that rules and regulations about the use of life science materials in their elementary classroom have been explained to students and that the most important information and safety facts have been posted.   _____
4. Allow pets into the elementary science classroom only upon written approval by a veterinarian; if pets are thus admitted, only the pet owner should be allowed to handle the animals.   _____
5. Reject all living or dead wild animals from the elementary science classroom.   _____
6. Explain the proper care procedures for keeping animals in the classroom. (These animals should be handled only by the teacher and should not be mistreated in any way by the elementary students.)   _____
7. Give complete directions to the elementary students as to the precautions to take regarding potential hazards they may encounter while working with life science materials in the classroom.   _____
8. Keep all hazardous materials related to life science materials in the elementary classroom in an adult lock-and-key situation.   _____
9. Emphasize that elementary students should not touch their eyes or skin or taste any material while working with plants, animals, or microorganisms.   _____
10. Provide constant supervision over all activities using life science materials.   _____
11. Require appropriate behavior of all students working with live materials.   _____

REFERENCES

Dean, Robert A.; Dean, Melanie Messer; and Motz, La Moine L. 1978. *Safety in the elementary classroom.* Prepared by the NSTA Sub-committee on Safety. Washington, D.C.: National Science Teachers Association.

Gerlovich, Jack, and Downs, Gary E. 1981. *Better science through safety.* Ames: Iowa State University Press.

Guiding principles in the use of animals by secondary school students and science club members. 1969. Washington, D.C.: National Society for Medical Research. July 1.

Grafton, Thurman F. 1979. Live animals for the biology classroom. *American Biology Teacher* 41 (7):410-12.

Harding, Delma E.; Volker, Roger P.; and Fagle, David L. 1969. *Creative biology teaching.* Ames: Iowa State University Press.

Holt, Bess-Gene. 1977. *Science with young children.* Washington, D.C.: National Association for the Education of Young Children.

Hone, Elizabeth V.; Joseph, Alexander; Victor, Edward; and Brandwein, Paul F. 1962. *A sourcebook for elementary science.* New York: Harcourt, Brace, and World.

Limburg, Peter R. 1976. *Poisonous plants.* New York: Simon and Schuster.

————. 1979. *Poisonous cultivated and wild plants.* Portland, Maine: Poison Control Center, Maine Medical Center.

Orlans, F. Barbara. 1977. *Animal care from protozoa to small mammals.* Menlo Park, Calif.: Addison-Wesley.

Science safety. 1976. Richmond, Va.: Department of Education, Commonwealth of Virginia.

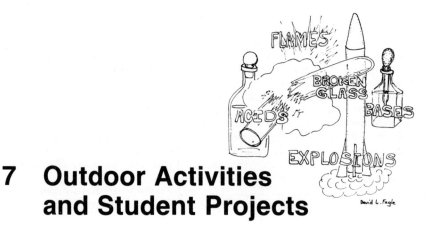

7 Outdoor Activities and Student Projects

David L. Fagle

OUTDOOR ACTIVITIES

Field trips, excursions, and out-of-classroom activities are indispensable components of instruction in the science education program of the elementary school. However, since such activities deviate from the regular patterns of classroom work, they may present serious hazards for the safety of students unless careful plans are made and possible difficulties anticipated. The nature of outdoor activities provides inherent opportunities for injury, more than in the familiar and controlled setting of the classroom. Most teachers are sensitive to this increased vulnerability; otherwise the accident rate on field trips probably would be higher.

Many outdoor activities may be carried out on the school ground or in areas nearby, thereby reducing schedule disruptions and hazards. These activities also demand planning and special techniques, but not to the same degree as do those conducted some distance away. Walking trips are easier to organize than those requiring transportation. School grounds are often overlooked as sites for field study, and teachers should consider the possibility of developing study sites there. Teachers should not avoid outdoor activities since many valuable outcomes can be achieved through them; rather, teachers should make functional use of field trips and recognize danger factors associated with them.

Advance Planning

Advance planning is necessary and one of the most important factors in avoiding accidents. A prerequisite for an outdoor science activity is the belief that it will be unique in meeting objectives of both teacher and students. Outdoor activities in the science program should be planned as all other lessons are planned, considering all phases, including specific objectives to be achieved, follow-up procedures, and evaluative processes.

Planning may prove that certain desirable aspects of a field trip will need to be curtailed or modified if unusual hazards for students are discovered. For example, a visit to a cave can be very valuable in studying adaptation of plants and animals, and high school and college classes may use a particular cave in the region for a variety of purposes. However, the same cave may not be suitable for elementary school students to visit. Planning should take into account the age and size of the students. Physical demands of walking, climbing, crawling, and other such feats may exceed the strength and endurance of young children.

Advance planning should include an inspection of sites to be visited before the activity occurs. If the site is some distance from the school, travel time should be checked. Maps and diagrams should be made and annotated, with special attention to sites with unusual hazards and cautions as well as the general routes to be followed and the various points of interest and instruction to be noted.

Consent and Permission
Standard procedures and forms should be developed on a system-wide basis to give information to all concerned as to the nature and location of the activity. Also, the forms may be used to secure necessary consent and information concerning such student health conditions as allergies, special medications, and physical limitations. When students in the activity use the school ground, only school authorities need to be informed and they may need to give official endorsement.

When the activity involves travel away from the school, certainly the administrative offices should give official consent; parents should be informed and should give written consent for student participation; and the health office should be notified. Authorities at the visitation site should also be contacted and asked to give written permission. This permission may be sought at the time of a preliminary visit by the teacher and each separate class visit should receive permission. Some sites may be visited repeatedly over a period of years and it may be judged that a preliminary visit is not always necessary. This preliminary visit may be omitted selectively because outdoor conditions change quickly. When permission at the visitation site is requested, additional supervision and instructional assistance may also be asked for. Authorities at the site may have some specific expectations that should be identified and carefully described for visitors. These should be included with the final instructions and schedules for the trip.

Transportation
School transportation should be used if at all possible when transportation is needed. School bus drivers are accustomed to transporting young children and it is quite likely that a number of the students in the class are accustomed to riding school buses. Drivers and students on the school bus know the expectations of behavior; however, since some of the students may not ride buses

regularly, the teacher should give explicit instructions for behavior, and the driver should emphasize these instructions at the beginning of the trip.

If private automobiles are to be used, the drivers and the teacher should agree upon expected behavior. Explicit rules involving teacher, driver, and students are important (for example, automobiles should not be overcrowded). Backup transportation should be available to avoid delays due to changes in plans or mechanical problems. For insurance purposes, it is important that school administrators know and sanction the use of personal vehicles for transporting students.

Supervision and Instruction

The degree of supervision needed for students is dependent upon their ages and maturity. It may be necessary to obtain teacher aides to accompany the students since outdoor activities require more adult supervision than classroom work does. Special provisions may need to be made for handicapped students and extra supervisors may well be needed. If student behavior is a problem, outdoor activities may have to be curtailed. Although such curtailment may diminish the quality of the educational program, inappropriate student behavior on a field trip often cancels the value of the experience and subjects everyone to increased vulnerability to accidents. The curtailment may involve only selected individuals but at times may have to be applied to the entire class.

Supervision should involve the development of a detailed activity schedule. As many as possible--teacher, aides, extra supervisors, consultants, and students--involved in the trip should participate in the development of the schedule. Once developed, the schedule should be shared widely and studied carefully in the classroom prior to the field trip. The possibility of unexpected events and emergencies must be provided for in the schedule. Each student should be paired with another student ("buddy system") so that in the event of an accident the uninjured student can secure help. There should be regular checkpoint times and identified mustering points included in the trip schedule.

Dress and Protective Gear

Appropriate clothing should be worn for the weather and the particular site to be visited. Parents' cooperation may be needed in ensuring proper dress. Correct footwear is important; open-toed sandals are not appropriate for outdoor science field experiences. Eye protection may need to be provided if a project such as rock study requires the use of a rock hammer or pick. All students should be encouraged to participate in supervised water studies, although it would probably be unwise to have large numbers of children in the water at one time. Those working close to bodies of water should have flotation vests and certainly those in water should wear them. Protective helmets should be used where there is the possibility of falling materials.

The health office should be asked to provide basic first aid

materials to be used in the case of accidents. Insect bites may be
a special hazard for some students. Information concerning allergic responses to outdoor conditions should be known about each student as a part of the student's classroom record; the parent's consent form might provide the identification of such a condition.
The health office should be consulted about procedures and medication to use with individuals requiring special attention.

Chapter 6, Life Sciences, describes precautions to observe in
studying plants and animals in the field as well as in the classroom. Collections in the field should be held to a minimum, for
both ecological and safety reasons. Showmanship in capturing wild
animals, on the part of either teachers or students, has no place
in field study.

Final Plan and Follow-up
    A written description and schedule of an outdoor activity
should be finished long enough before the planned date so it can be
studied in class and distributed to all involved. As stated above,
the plan should be developed with input from as many participants
as possible. The plan should include the following components:

 1. purpose of the trip
 2. specific learning objectives
 3. time schedule with permissible deviations noted
 4. method of transportation
 5. statement as to behavior during transportation
 6. special clothing
 7. special protective clothing and gear
 8. equipment and supplies
 9. first aid materials
10. grouping of pupils for activities
11. specific tasks of individual study groups
12. aides to work with study groups
13. maps and diagrams of study sites with identification of poten-
     tial hazards
14. directions to follow in the event of emergencies and change of
     schedule
15. identification of mustering points
16. outline of activities in which groups will participate during
     transportation, particularly if trip is of considerable dura-
     tion
17. list of things to identify enroute
18. description of follow-up activities
19. evaluation of the activities

    Provision should be made for modification of plans if the trip
must be cancelled or if the schedule must be changed. A telephone
network may be established, if one does not already exist for the
class, in order for information to be shared.

    It is important that each outdoor activity have a follow-up
that integrates it with the overall program of study. This follow-

up may take a variety of forms and extend from the conclusion of
the activity over several weeks in which data and material col-
lected may be used for analysis and study.

An important part of the follow-up will be evaluation by all
involved. Attention should be given to the safety aspects of the
trip and modifications to be made in the future to improve safety
factors.

DRILLS AND EMERGENCY PROCEDURES

Just as fire drills and tornado drills are important for elementary classes, so are drills as to what should be done in the
field when emergencies arise. Drills, depending upon the nature of
the particular activity, should include the following: reporting
accidents; first aid in the event of serious lacerations, broken
bones, snake bites, drowning, and fainting; identification of poisonous plants or other materials to avoid in the field; behavior
when outdoors in a lightning storm or other dangerous weather condition; and emergency evacuation of a bus or other vehicle used for
transportation.

The general point of view suggested for improving the safety
conditions for outdoor activities is that if they are well planned,
if students are involved in the planning, if they are used as integral parts of the educational program, and if they lead to valuable learning experiences, the vulnerability of students to accidents and emergencies in such activities will be reduced. Quality
outdoor education provides for quality safety education in the out-
of-doors.

STUDENT PROJECTS

Safety measures to be used with student projects should be appropriate for the specific project and for the motor development,
knowledge, and desire of the student. A project undertaken by a
second grader would require much different precautions, desired
practices, and limitations than would a project being done by a
sixth grader. Only a few general statements are made here.

Design

All student projects (individual or group) should be designed
in consultation with the teacher. The teacher should focus on possible hazards to anticipate, and the safety measures to take to
avoid or deal with these hazards. Any independent study contract or
project should include safety considerations as an integral part of
its design.

The teacher will need to make sure that the design meets all
appropriate codes governing the use of scientific materials and
that students always treat animals humanely. Guidelines for such
treatment may be obtained from the American Association for the
Advancement of Science (AAAS), 1515 Massachusetts Ave., N.W., Washington, D.C. 20005.

The teacher should give special attention to the safety factors involved in the project as the design is discussed and approved and should not approve a particular project until adequate student attention has been given to these safety factors.

Supervision

All projects done by students should emphasize safety of the participants, other persons in the near vicinity, and the public in general.

Many projects appropriate at the junior high or senior high level would be inappropriate for students at the elementary level. The teacher should always consider the knowledge, psychomotor skills, and processes required of students to work with projects safely. Some projects, although not prohibited entirely, might require special equipment and special supervision. It is possible, on *some occasions*, for elementary projects to be supervised by experts not employed by the school. A student might work with high school science teachers, university professors, physicians, engineers, or other highly trained experts. However, the elementary teacher should be *totally cognizant* of the activities being done and ensure that the activities are performed when the experts are with the students.

Home Laboratory

The elementary teacher of science *cannot and should not take responsibility for laboratories established in the home.* Projects expected as part of the regular class work or those sponsored by the school should be conducted almost exclusively at the school. On special occasions some parents may desire to assume supervision of certain projects because of their own expertise. On all such occasions it is recommended that the classroom teacher have the parent(s) provide (in writing) a willingness to assume all responsibilities for such school-related activities.

Many activity-oriented projects have some degree of risk involved. The teacher must be knowledgeable of dangers inherent in performing these activities and always be a "future-oriented" teacher concerning safety aspects. Being future-oriented in reference to possible dangerous and/or problem activities will eliminate most accidents or near accidents.

CHECKLIST

1. Visit proposed sites and know about the potential
   hazards and areas to be avoided.   _____
2. Use proper consent and permission forms prior to
   outdoor activities.   _____
3. Use appropriate school, or school endorsed,
   transportation.   _____
4. Arrange for adequate supervision for planned
   activities.   _____

5. Ensure appropriate student dress and protective
   gear needed for the activities.
6. Plan procedures to follow in case of emergencies.   _____
7. Use appropriate procedures in project design.   _____
8. Know the kinds of supervision necessary for
   different student projects.   _____
9. Know the procedures to follow for home laboratory activities.   _____

REFERENCES

Gerlovich, Jack A., and Downs, Gary E. 1981. *Better science
    through safety*. Ames: Iowa State University Press.
North Carolina Department of Public Instruction. 1977. *Safety
    first in science teaching*. New York: Holt, Rinehart, and
    Winston.
Sweetser, Evan A. Field trips and teacher liability. 1974. *Amer-
    ican Biology Teacher* 36 (4):239-40.

David L. Fagle

8 Science Safety for Handicapped Students

Schools have become much more concerned about the education of students with handicaps since PL94-142 and Section 504 of the Vocational Rehabilitation Act were passed. These federal laws dictate that handicapped students must be educated in the least restrictive environment, which means that many of these students will be enrolled in the regular classroom for the first time. Most teachers have had experience with the temporarily handicapped student, that is, the student with the broken leg or arm or some other short-term malady from which the student usually recovers completely. However, many teachers have not had to deal with handicapped students on an everyday basis for an entire school year.

The handicapped student in the elementary school science class has several difficulties. First, science is not a strong teaching area for many elementary teachers. Second, since science experiments are not done on a regular basis in many elementary classrooms, teachers are apt to be unfamiliar with the use of the equipment and other materials. Moreover, most elementary classrooms are not adapted well for science instruction, let alone adapted for a handicapped student participating in the class. The problem facing both teacher and student is to ensure that the student gains as much from the science experience as is possible and does it as safely as possible.

Although many articles and manuals have described safety rules and procedures for making the science class a safe environment, the safety of handicapped students has not been addressed in most of the materials reviewed. There must be a higher level of concern for handicapped students because they may not be able to see or hear dangerous situations developing, and, even if they do perceive a dangerous situation, they may not be able to react quickly enough to avoid the danger.

Since most elementary teachers have had little experience in teaching handicapped students, a few words on this topic are in

order. The general types of handicaps that may be present in the
classroom are hearing impairments, visual impairments, speech and
language impairments, learning disabilities, slight mental retardation, emotional disturbances, and ailments that require special
medication, braces, prostheses, or wheelchairs.

Since handicapped students want to be as normal as possible,
it is extremely important that the teacher treat them as normally
as possible, using the same grading and discipline for them as for
the rest of the class. It is the teacher's responsibility to find
good alternative experiences that the student might need. The
abilities of these students should never be underestimated or over-
estimated. The former will cause underachievement while the latter
will cause frustration if allowed to happen frequently. An article
in *Science Teacher* gives many suggestions for teachers to use in
integrating the handicapped child into the regular classroom (Bybee
1979). Pertinent sections of this article are included (with permission) at the end of this chapter.

What physical facilities are needed for the elementary science
student with a handicap? For the student in a wheelchair a special
table should be constructed so that the wheelchair can slide under
it easily. According to the wheelchair specifications in *Standards
for Making Buildings Intended for Use by the General Public Accessible to and Functional for the Physically Handicapped*, Iowa State
Building Code, Division 7, Section 5.703(1), most wheelchair models
have armrests 29 in. (74 cm) from the floor and are 25 in. (64 cm)
wide and 42 in. (107 cm) long. Hence an allowance of 30 in. (76
cm) from the floor to the bottom of the work surface would be desirable. Since the wheelchair is 25 in. (64 cm) wide, this means
that the opening under the table should be approximately 30 in.
(76 cm) wide. The opening under the table should be 18 in. (46 cm)
to 20 in. (51 cm) or more deep. The aisles between tables should
be at least 36 in. (81 cm) wide to accommodate wheelchair movement
easily.

Most elementary science experiments use chemicals or materials
that are not considered to be dangerous when properly used. However, some materials are considered dangerous under certain circumstances and all students, especially the handicapped, must be protected. The wheelchair user is sitting; hence spills are apt to go
in the lap. An explosion or test tube boilout could hit the student in the face or chest. For protection under these conditions,
it is recommended that the student wear an approved full face and
neck shield as well as an appropriate body cover. Students with
prosthetic limbs, artificial hands, hooks, or other artificial body
parts might need help in putting on and removing their protective
devices. Students who tire easily need to have chairs or stools
handy. Heating devices other than candles or alcohol burners
should be used by handicapped students; electric heating devices
with indicator lights are recommended.

One of the greatest helps in integrating the handicapped student is to have another student as a partner. Any student chosen
must be willing to help the handicapped student and not be easily

irritated if the partner progresses slowly. For some activities students may need to go through the procedure first to see how it is done before they actually do the activity.

The handicapped student will probably not be able to do all the activities expected of nonhandicapped students. In such cases the activity should be modified or another relevant experience substituted. The classroom teacher's common sense must be the final determiner of what is workable while following the mandate of PL94-142 and Section 504.

The following material from *Science Teacher* (Bybee 1979, 23-24) gives some guidelines that teachers may wish to use in working with handicapped students.

Understanding Special Students--General Guidelines
Certainly there are unique problems in integrating any special student into the classroom. Nevertheless, there are simple straightforward approaches that have proven helpful with most students:
• Obtain and read all the background information available on the student;
• Spend time educating yourself on the physical and/or psychological nature of the handicap, and how it affects the student's potential for learning;
• Determine whether or not special help can be made available to you through the resources of a "special education" expert;
• Determine any special equipment needed by the student;
• Talk with the student about limitations due to his or her handicap and about particular needs in the science class;
• Establish a team of fellow teachers (including resource teachers and aides) to share information and ideas about the special students. A team approach is helpful in overcoming initial fears and the sense of aloneness in dealing with the problem. You may need to take responsibility for contacting appropriate school personnel and establishing the team;
• Other students are often willing to help special students. Use them;
• Be aware of barriers--both physical and psychological--to the fullest possible functioning of the special student;
• Consider how to modify or adapt curriculum materials and teaching strategies for the special student without sacrificing content;
• Do not underestimate the capabilities of the special student. Teachers' perceptions of a student's abilities have a way of becoming self-fulfilling prophecies. If these perceptions are negative, they may detrimentally affect the student and your ability to create new options for him or her.
• Use the same standards of grading and discipline for the special student as you do for the rest of the class;
• Develop a trusting relationship with the special student;

● Educate the other students about handicaps in general, as
well as specific handicaps of students in their class.

Hearing Impaired
● The hearing impaired depend heavily on visual perception.
Therefore, seat the student for optimal viewing;
● Determine whether an interpreter will be needed and the na-
ture of the child's speech/language problems;
● Learn the child's most effective way of communicating;
● Find the student a "listening helper."

Visually Impaired
● Visually impaired students learn through sensory channels
other than vision, primarily hearing. Therefore, seat students for optimal listening.
● Determine from the student what constitutes the best lighting;
● Change the room arrangement whenever necessary, but always
make a special effort formally and informally to reorient
the student;
● Allow the student to manipulate tangible materials, models,
and when possible "real" objects. Do not unduly "protect"
students from materials;
● Speak aloud what you have written on the board and charts;
● Use the student's name; otherwise, the student may not know
when he or she is being addressed;
● Since smiles and facial gestures might not be seen, touching
is the most effective means of reinforcing the student's
work;
● Be aware of student eye fatigue. This can be overcome by
varying activities, using good lighting, and providing close
visual work.

Physically and Health Impaired
● Eliminate architectural barriers;
● Become familiar with the basic mechanics and maintenance of
braces, prostheses, and wheelchairs;
● Understand the effects of medication on students and know
the dosage;
● Obtain special devices such as pencil holders or reading
aids for students who need them;
● Learn about the symptoms of special health problems, and
appropriate responses.

Speech and Language Impaired
● Help the student become aware of his or her problem; students must be able to hear their own errors;
● Incorporate and draw attention to newly learned sounds in
familiar words;
● Know what to listen for, and match appropriate remediation
exercises with the student's problem;

• Be sure your speech is articulate; students often develop speech and language patterns through modeling.

Learning Disabilities and Mental Retardation
• Listen closely so you can understand the student's perception and understanding of concepts and procedures;
• Use an individualized approach based on the student's learning style, level of understanding, and readiness;
• Use multisensory approaches to learning: visual, auditory, kinesthetic, and tactile;
• Find and use the student's most refined sensory mode to aid in development of mental capacities;
• Teach to the student's strengths, and work on diminishing his or her deficiencies;
• Reduce or control interruptions since many special students have short attention spans;
• Stay within the student's limits of frustration. Rely on your judgment, not the level of curriculum materials;
• Start conceptual development at a sensory-motor or concrete level, and work toward more abstract levels;
• Work on speech and language development;
• Help special students to develop self-esteem; a good, firmly grounded self-concept is essential to their continued development.

Emotionally Disturbed and Disruptive Students
• Make rules reasonable and clear;
• Provide realistic, appropriate consequences if rules are broken;
• Never use physical punishment for rule violation;
• Disruptive behavior ranges from low levels at which a student may merely be looking for attention or recognition through a spectrum that ends in rage, tantrums, or complete withdrawal. Try always to be alert to behaviors that, though minimally disruptive, could become more serious problems;
• Resolve conflicts by talking and reasoning with the student. Once a course toward aggressive or uncontrolled behavior is started, it is hard to stop;
• If behavior problems escalate, try to talk about the process while providing ways out of the problem. For example, "We are both getting angry, can't we settle this calmly," or "I see you are upset, let's try to solve the problem."

CHECKLIST

1. Be aware of laws that relate to the education of handicapped students.   _____
2. Be knowledgeable about problems that face ele-

mentary teachers in teaching science to handicapped learners.
3. Be knowledgeable about physical facilities needed
   for the elementary handicapped science student.   _____
4. Know what to do to protect handicapped students.   _____
5. Be knowledgeable about guidelines that may be
   used in working with handicapped students.   _____

REFERENCES

Bybee, Roger. 1979. Helping the special student fit in. *Science
    Teacher* 46(3):23-24.
Crowder, Betty Pogue, et al. 1977. *Reference guide for elementary
    science*, ED 174472. Pontiac, Mich.: Oakland County Schools.
Gerlovich, Jack, and Downs, Gary E. 1981. *Better science through
    safety*. Ames: Iowa State University Press.
Hofman, Helenmarie H. 1978. *A working conference on science edu-
    cation for handicapped students*. Washington, D.C.: National
    Science Teachers Association. (Contains large bibliography.)
Hofman, Helenmarie H., and Ricker, Kenneth S. 1979. *Science edu-
    cation and the physically handicapped*. Washington, D.C.:
    National Science Teachers Association.
Science education news. Fall 1978/Winter 1979. Washington, D.C.:
    American Association for the Advancement of Science. (Con-
    tains large bibliography.)
Willoughby, Doris, ed. 1979. *Your school includes a blind stu-
    dent*. Chatsworth, Calif.: National Federation of the Blind,
    Teachers Division.
Yukers, Harold E.; Revenson, Joyce; and Fracchia, John F. 1968.
    *The modification of education equipment and curriculum for
    maximum utilization by physically disabled persons*, ED 031022.
    Albertson, N.Y.: Human Resources Center.

The following organizations can provide additional information:

American Foundation for the Blind, Inc., 15 West 16th Street,
New York, NY 10011.
American Printing House for the Blind, Inc., 1839 Frankfort
Ave., Louisville, KY 40206.
Association for Education of the Visually Handicapped, 919
Walnut Street, Philadelphia, PA 19107.
Division for the Visually Handicapped, Council for Exceptional
Children, 1920 Association Dr., Reston, VA 22091.
National Federation of the Blind, 1800 Johnson St., Baltimore,
MD 21202.
National Society for the Prevention of Blindness, 79 Madison
Ave., New York, NY 10016.

9 Physical Plant Facilities

From elementary grades through the universities greater emphasis is being placed on functional science instruction, which involves relationships among various science disciplines. Toxic or flammable chemicals, pathogens, carcinogens, contagious and/or infectious agents, and greater use of animals on practically all levels of the science curriculum make consciousness of the role of safety imperative in science education. Principles of safety used in a science setting will carry over to the home in many cases. It is inherent, then, that the instructor can and should mention these carryovers consistently.

There are two basic considerations for safety in science education: first, the physical surroundings and their conduciveness to safety; and second, the role of the science teacher. The elementary classroom should be designed with the major desired learning outcomes in mind, including the development of basic skills, opportunities to exercise these skills in meaningful situations, and the promotion of physical, social, and emotional growth of the learner. The elementary classroom is affected by the use of television, audiovisual aids, and team, or coordinated, teaching. Most programs point to the need for fairly large and flexible space. The teacher is responsible for taking leadership in demonstrating and correlating safety practices in the utilization of various science concepts, thereby making safety education an integral part of the science education program.

CLASSROOMS

Classrooms approaching a square, rectangle, or circle seem particularly well adapted to providing a desirable environment for elementary learning activities; however, the final shape of the room should be determined by the outcome of the planning process and the kinds of activities to be encompassed.

Based on maximum room occupancy of 30 students, 900 to 960 sq ft of floor area should be provided in a self-contained classroom that includes work counters and storage spaces. This amounts to 30-32 sq ft per student, and can go as high as 40-45 sq ft per student--or higher if more flexibility is desired.

Some school planners would include instructional areas of varied sizes, adjacent to each other by means of operable dividers. The combination of these spaces would permit team, or coordinated, teaching; interest spaces; laboratory spaces for small to large groups; or extension of a particular area. The smaller spaces would also serve for small group instructional activities. *Flexibility* is the key to the planning process and successful space utilization.

Generally, elementary classrooms are self-contained facilities except for such services as a library/media center, gymnasium, or school lunchroom. Classrooms generally include, but are not limited to, the following areas:

1. General instructional areas.
2. Facilities for language arts, mathematics, social studies. These largely involve the general instructional area, wall space, some equipment and storage (maps, charts, etc.).
3. Facilities for science, art, music, and crafts. These may involve some supplementary space and will require specialized equipment and storage.
4. Teacher center. Desk and chair(s) in general instructional area.

SPECIAL FACILITIES NEEDED

Elementary students acquire science facts and concepts by many types of media, by communication, and by hands-on process skills. The elementary school classroom should therefore be equipped with special facilities to permit a variety of learning techniques. Such facilities for science in the classroom will not deter but rather will aid the instruction in other areas. This is particularly true when science is an integrated part of the total learning experience.

The classroom should contain (but not be limited to) the following:

1. Demonstration table, mobile--for teacher use. The usual type is a portable table, preferably on lockable casters, with a chemically resistant top, a small stainless sink with a pump faucet, fresh-water and waste tanks (polyethylene), shelves (possibly with trays), and a grounded electrical receptacle with connecting cord. The table should be high enough that pupils may easily see the demonstrations. The sink, pump faucet, and fresh-water and waste tanks must be in proper working order and not leaking.
2. Work table for children. One or more tables should be pro-

vided where students may sit or stand, handle materials, and receive instruction. A movable table (with or without lockable casters), either rectangular or circular, with a chemical- and heat-resistant top is preferred. It is better in some ways to have students work around movable tables rather than fixed tables. Additional table space is required for the use of tools. It is recommended that students not sit down when doing activities that could result in spillage of liquids in their laps.

3. Wall-counter unit. A fixed wall-counter unit with shelves, doors, and drawers, and a water and sink unit is becoming standard equipment in elementary classroom construction. This provides a work area, display space, and storage space. The wall-counter unit should be covered with a heat- and chemical-resistant material, such as formica, and should be at least 20 in. (51 cm) wide. If wall counters are to be provided, they should be the correct height for student use and constructed so that students will not be allowed to sit at benches while conducting experiments.

4. Special items. The following items also need special consideration for a science program:
   a) Electrical supply. An adequate number of circuits should be provided and properly grounded. The use of ground fault intercepters will aid in preventing electrical shock.
   b) Ventilation. Normal ventilation of classrooms will generally suffice. When noxious materials are in use, a portable fume hood is recommended. The laboratory ventilation system must effectively remove airborne harmful gases and also exhaust a minimum volume of air. Additional air should be supplied to laboratories to replace air removed by exhaust; air should not be recirculated. Fume hoods should be vented directly to the outside.
   c) Water and sink. Both hot and cold water are desirable. The sink should be deep to prevent back-splash and should be trapped.
   d) Storage. Adequate storage of various types should be provided:
      ● open storage for display purposes, and for some equipment and supplies.
      ● closed storage for chemicals and equipment. Must be lockable for potentially dangerous chemicals.
      ● flameproof storage if flammable materials are used and stored.
      ● special storage for eye protective devices. Proper sanitation of eye protective devices also needs to be considered.
   e) Lighting. A minimum of 50 fc of light must be available at the working surface.
   f) Floor coverings. These should be heat and chemical resistant as well as nonskid where students will be working on projects.

g) Eye wash. This must be located in any room where chemicals
are used. It can be of various types. (See the Appendix,
p. 123, in *Better science through safety* for a photograph of
this equipment.)

LABORATORY CENTER
     Certain types of equipment and materials may be shared by a
number of classrooms in the elementary school. The central storage
room or laboratory center provides for the keeping of such equipment. The laboratory center should be accessible to all teachers,
and equipment should be taken from the center to individual rooms
according to established policies. Shared equipment ordinarily
found at the center may include electrical meters, a microprojec-
tor, microscopes, a motion picture projector, an opaque projector,
film and filmstrips, models, a planetarium, a telescope, vacuum-
pressure pumps, and other like equipment as well as stock quantities of materials and supplies.
     In those schools where teaching of science is the responsibil-
ity of a specialist, a laboratory may be provided. This laboratory
should be equipped so that a minimum of 4 sq ft of mar-resistant
working space is available for each child. The number of electrical and gas outlets, storage cupboards, open shelves for equipment
and books, window shelves, aquarium tables, and display cabinets
and/or shelves needed in the laboratory will be estimated best by
the science specialist, who should be consulted before remodeling
or construction is undertaken. Each laboratory should have dark-
room shades and at least one sink. In some instances, a demonstration table equipped with a sink, an electrical outlet, a gas outlet, and a support stand for suspending certain items for apparatus
will also be useful.

FIRE SAFETY
1. Fire extinguishers. Every classroom in which science experi-
    mentation or demonstration takes place should have a proper
    fire extinguisher located in the room. Generally the multi-
    rated A-B-C type is recommended.
2. Fire blanket. Every classroom where an open flame is used
    should also be equipped with an appropriate fire blanket.
3. Fire-safe storage for flammable materials that may be used in
    the elementary science program. This can be provided in con-
    tainers or in a cabinet either purchased or made according to
    specifications. (Building specifications may be found in *Bet-
    ter science through safety*, 124.)

CHECKLIST

1. Know if a fire extinguisher
    • is in the room;   _____

- is properly charged and tagged;
- is accessible.
2. Know how to properly operate the fire extinguisher.
3. Know where to place and how to use an eye wash station.
4. Be able to
   - identify some auxiliary type ventilation;
   - determine whether the auxiliary ventilation works properly (grills are clean and free from dirt);
   - determine where exhausted air goes.
5. Be able to check the proper operation of a sink (both hot and cold water).
6. Check the classroom for sufficient electrical outlets.
7. Check for lockable storage for potentially dangerous chemicals and materials.
8. Check for proper storage of flammable materials.
9. Be knowledgeable about proper sanitation and storage of eye protective devices.
10. Know the proper type(s) of floor(s) needed for conducting the science program.
11. Be aware of the proper lighting necessary for student activities.
12. Know how to locate and use a master valve for gas and a master control for electricity.
13. Make sure all emergency routes are posted in the classroom.
14. Know how to check for and change room facilities to accommodate handicapped learners.

REFERENCES

Christian, Floyd R. 1968. *Safety in the science laboratory: A guide.* Tallahassee, Fla.: State Department of Education.

Guidelines for sites, facilities, and equipment. 1974. Des Moines: Iowa Department of Public Instruction, School Facilities Unit.

McDermoth, John J. 1975. A budgetwise science laboratory. *Science and Children* 13(3):25-27.

Richardson, John S. *School facilities for science instruction.* Washington, D.C.: National Science Teachers Association.

Walters, Lou. 1972. Elementary school science facility. *Science and Children* 9(8):8-10.

David L. Fagle

10 Fire Protection and Control

Elementary school students should learn about the principles of heat and temperature and about fire and fire control. *Heat* is energy that passes from one place of higher temperature to another place of lower temperature. Temperature is not a measure of how much heat is in an object. *Temperature* only tells which way heat will flow. Heat always flows from places of higher temperature to places of lower temperature.

The term *hot* is an interesting one. When we say an object, or place, is hot, we usually mean that it is at a temperature above a stated or implied temperature. Hot is thus a relative term really meaning hotter.

Heat energy is obtained by conversion from one or more of the other energy forms: light, motion (mechanical), chemical, electrical, and nuclear. The two commonest controlled sources of heat are electrical and chemical (burning of fuels in fires).

Since heat is always moving from places at given temperatures to other places at lower temperatures, many observations of the principles of heat and temperature can be made without using fire or electric heaters. For example, body temperature is above room temperature, the temperatures near the radiators or registers of the room heating system are higher than in the rest of the room, and the temperatures near windows may be higher due to solar heating. These relative temperature differences can be used in teaching activities.

CLASSROOM HEAT SOURCES

Two paramount rules are to be followed when using heat in elementary level science classes.

1. Never use fire (open flame) unless absolutely necessary! Consider all other methods first.
2. When fire (open flame) is used it must be under direct, continuous teacher supervision and control.

Concepts of heat and temperature are related to temperature differences. Heat from the sun and from the building's heating system should be used if possible. When higher temperatures are needed, consider electric heaters first. The heat from a common electric light bulb may be all that is needed. A gooseneck lamp with a hemispheric shade reflector is a good heat source. Teachers should use sources of heat such as these, which, although they may provide heat slowly, are safer than open flames.

Heat sources in order of acceptability in the elementary school classroom may be divided into three groups:

Level 1—solar, body, building- or room-heating systems
Level 2—electrical heating devices: light bulbs, heat lamps, electric heaters
Level 3—solid fuel sources: sterno-type cartridges, candles

Alcohol lamps are not recommended since their liquid fuel is highly flammable; flame detection is difficult; they are easily tipped; and they are dangerous to light, use, and control.

Electrical heating devices should be in good condition and should have automatic shutoff switches that operate when the device is tipped.

A simple way to heat water is in an electric coffeepot or teapot. It should be operated on a flat, sturdy table or on the floor, and against a wall well away from student traffic.

Bunsen burners and other such heat sources may be used when high temperatures are needed but these should be used only by the teacher. The stability of the setup is crucial! Propane torches may also be used following the manufacturers' suggestions and precautions.

When individual students or small groups each need a heat source, solid fuel heaters (such as Sterno) may be used, following the manufacturer's suggestions and precautions. The number of such heaters should be kept to a minimum. If the students work in groups, one of each group can be designated to be the Fire Monitor; this person lights and extinguishes the flame and monitors the others for safe actions. Each group should have a shallow aluminum dish with wet sand in it. Used matches can be placed in the sand to ensure that each is extinguished.

The use of candles is sometimes necessary. Candles should be 1 in. (2.5 cm) or more in diameter and not over 2 in. (5 cm) high. Wax may be dripped into an aluminum dish to anchor the candle and moist sand placed around the candle in the bottom.

Students must exercise care with solar heaters. While passive in nature, solar heaters in the proper position can concentrate light rays and cause burns or fires.

WHEN A FIRE OCCURS

The teacher's first concern is the safety of the children! At the first sign of fire:

1. Direct the children to leave the room.
2. Set off the fire alarm.
3. Call the fire department.

The teacher should direct and supervise the orderly departure of the students following the emergency drill procedures in effect in the school. Send one trustworthy student to sound the alarm. Send another student to the school office to report the emergency and call the fire department. If the office is at some distance and an outside phone is nearer, a third student, or an adult s/he may encounter, can place the call to the fire department.

Do not attempt to extinguish the fire until the above three steps have been attended to!

Be prepared. Set up, in advance, a system to make sure that steps (2) and (3) can be done quickly and surely. Train students to do these. Have them practice. Appoint them as Fire Monitors or some similar title.

Do not hesitate on these steps. It is better to err on the side of safety!

FIRE SAFETY

All fires require three things: something that will burn (the fuel), oxygen (present in air), and a source of ignition. It is the ignition source that brings a fuel up to its kindling temperature. This is the lowest temperature at which a flame can be maintained.

Fires are extinguished by removing any one of the three essentials. The commonest method is to apply water, which cools whatever is burning below its kindling temperature. However, for certain chemical, metal, and electrical fires, extinguishing by water is not appropriate. Refer to Figure 10.1 for the appropriate class extinguisher.

Fire safety may be thought of in terms of which factor is the critical one--that is, the last one to be joined with the other two. Since oxygen and flammable materials are nearly always present, it is a spark or open flame that usually ignites them, causing fire. Thus one should be constantly alert to sparks or open flames.

The other two factors must be kept in mind also, however. A small fire can become a larger one if fanned by a breeze that supplies more oxygen. A student's clothing, hair, or papers may catch

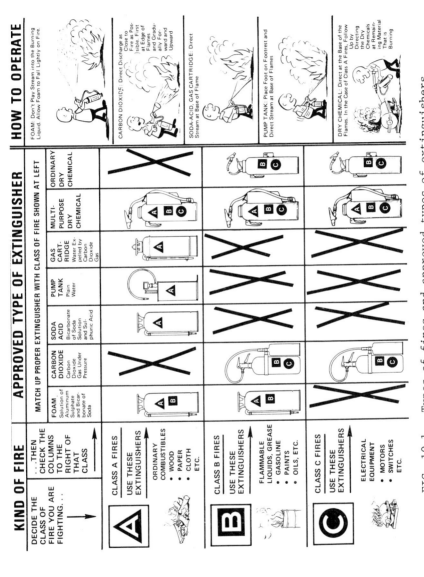

FIG. 10.1. Types of fires and approved types of extinguishers. (From National Institute for Occupational Safety and Health.)

fire if these "fuels" are brought into contact with an open flame or spark.

EXTINGUISHING A FIRE

Once the three emergency steps have been taken, and the children's safety is assured, it is time to pay attention to the fire.

Remove sources of ignition and fuel. Shut off gas. Disconnect electrical devices. Move paper, cloth, other flammable materials away from the fire.

Use the fire extinguisher. Ideally this will be a Tri-Class (A,B,C) dry chemical extinguisher. These use a multipurpose dry chemical suitable for use on all fires. Refer to Figure 10.1 for additional information on types of fires and suitability of various types of extinguishers. Be familiar with the type supplied to your room or school.

Each classroom should have an approved fire blanket in a clearly marked cabinet or container. One or two large bath towels are also useful for emergency fire blankets. If hair or clothing catches fire, roll the victim up in the blanket or towel. Do not swat or fan the fire! Smother it quickly.

A supply of sand is also useful for smothering small fires. It may be kept in plastic (ice cream) containers clearly marked in red.

SOME DO'S AND DON'TS

1. Do instruct all students in fire safety rules.
2. Do train a cadre of Fire Monitors.
3. Do use CO_2 gas only on electrical fires.
4. Do have students restrain loose hair and clothing.
5. Do use only 6-12 volt electrical devices (except for heating).
6. *Do study Figure 10.1.*
7. Don't put thermometers in flame.
8. Don't heat flammable liquids over an open flame.
9. Don't build or use chemical volcanoes.
10. Don't short-circuit batteries.

CHECKLIST

1. Know what kinds of classroom heat sources to use. _____
2. Know what procedures to follow if a fire should occur. _____
3. Know what three components are necessary to have a fire. _____
4. Know the appropriate type of fire extinguisher to use. _____
5. Possess working knowledge of fire extinguishers. _____

11   First Aid

The goal of any safety program is to prevent accidents rather than treat them. If this goal were universally achieved, there would be no need for a first aid section in this publication. However, accidents and illnesses do occur, and first aid treatment in such situations must be a consideration of a safety program.

WHAT IS FIRST AID?

First aid is the immediate care given to a person who has been injured or taken ill suddenly. It includes well-selected words of encouragement, evidence of willingness to help, and promotion of confidence by demonstration of competence.

In cases of serious injury or sudden illness, while help is being summoned, immediate attention should be given to these first aid priorities:

1. Effect a prompt rescue (for example, remove an accident victim from a room containing carbon monoxide gas or other toxic fumes).
2. Ensure that the victim has an open airway, and give mouth-to-mouth artificial respiration if necessary.
3. Control severe bleeding.
4. Give first aid for poisoning, or for ingestion of any harmful substances.

Teachers should be encouraged to avail themselves of the first aid training courses that might be offered in their communities.

Much material in this section was derived (with permission) from *American Red Cross standard first aid and personal safety.* 1979. Garden City, N.Y.: Doubleday. Large portions also appear in *Better science through safety*, pp. 131-41.

All persons giving first aid should know the limits of their capabilities and make every effort to avoid further injury to the victim in attempts to provide the best possible emergency first aid care, doing only what is deemed absolutely necessary and leaving the diagnosis and treatment to trained medical people. It is recommended that teachers learn early in the school year the potentially dangerous medical/health problems their students may have.

COURSES AVAILABLE

American Red Cross
Noninstructor Courses: Hours:
    Standard First Aid and Personal Safety   14
    Standard First Aid--Multimedia System   7 1/2
    Cardiopulmonary Resuscitation (CPR)   6
Instructor Courses:
    Standard First Aid--Multimedia System   1
    Orientation on CPR   2 1/2
Address:
    American Red Cross, Iowa Division
    2116 Grand Avenue
    Des Moines, IA   50312
    Phone: (515) 243-7681
In other states contact the state Red Cross chapter.

Iowa Heart Association
Noninstructor Courses:
    Cardiopulmonary Resuscitation (CPR)
        Heart Saver Course   4
        Basic Rescuer Course   7-9
Instructor Courses:
    CPR Contact association for information.
Address:
    Iowa Heart Association
    1111 Office Park Road
    West Des Moines, IA   50265
    Phone: (515) 224-1025, (800) 422-3144
In other states contact the state Heart Association office.

School personnel who have received first aid training and who are faced with a medical emergency must assess the status of the accident prior to taking any action. They should ask themselves the following questions: What first aid can I provide? Which injuries are true medical emergencies requiring immediate first aid? Which victims may be moved?

TRANSPORTATION OF VICTIMS
It should be recognized that more harm can be done through improper rescue and transportation than through any other measures associated with emergency assistance.

Unless there is immediate danger to life, victims should not be transported until such life-threatening problems as airway obstruction and hemorrhage are cared for and wounds are dressed.

Most schools are located where rescue services, ambulances, and other medical support services are readily available. The wise first aider will use those services in preference to using makeshift transportation procedures.

TRAUMATIC SHOCK

Traumatic shock (reduced blood volume and pressure) may result from serious injuries of all kinds: hemorrhage or loss of body fluids, heart attack, burns, poisoning by chemicals, gases, alcohol, or drugs. Shock also results from lack of oxygen caused by obstruction of air passages or injury to the respiratory system. Shock is aggravated by pain, by rough handling, and by delay in treatment. If untreated, it can result in death to the victim.

Symptoms include pale, cold, clammy skin; weakness; rapid pulse; shallow and rapid breathing; and nausea.

Recommended treatment:

1. Keep victims lying down.
2. Cover victims only enough to prevent loss of body heat.
3. Get medical help as soon as possible.
4. Victims having difficulty breathing may be placed on their backs with head and shoulders raised.
5. Victims may improve if the feet are raised from 8 to 12 in. Lower the feet back to a level position if any difficulty in breathing or additional pain results.
6. If medical attention will be delayed for more than one-half hour, small amounts of fluids may be given a victim who is conscious. Lukewarm water is usually the most available.

ARTIFICIAL RESPIRATION

The objectives of artificial respiration are to maintain an open airway through the mouth, nose, or stoma (tracheotomy victims) and to restore breathing by maintaining an alternating increase and decrease in the expansion of the chest.

Recovery is usually rapid except in cases involving carbon monoxide poisoning, drug overdose, or electrical shock.

Artificial respiration should be continued until victims start to breathe for themselves or until a medical authority assumes responsibility or pronounces them dead.

The mouth-to-mouth method:

1. Clear any foreign matter from the mouth.
2. Tilt the head back to open the air passage. Make sure the chin is pointing upward.
3. Pinch the nostrils shut with thumb and index finger.
4. Blow air into the mouth. Your mouth should be open wide and sealed tightly around the mouth of the victim.

5.   Stop blowing when the chest is expanded. Remove your mouth.
     Turn your head and listen for exhalation. Watch the chest to
     see that it falls.
6.   Repeat the cycle 12 times per min (every 5 sec).
7.   Get medical assistance.

HEIMLICH MANEUVER
     An effective way to remove an object blocking the windpipe is
the Heimlich maneuver. To perform this maneuver:

1.   Stand behind the victim and place your arms around the victim's
     waist.
2.   Make a fist and place it so that the thumb is against the abdo-
     men slightly above the navel and below the ribcage.
3.   Grasp your fist with the other hand and then press your fist
     into the abdomen with a quick upward thrust.

     This action forces air out of the lungs and blows the object
from the windpipe.
     If the victim has collapsed or is too large for you to support
or place your arms around:

1.   Place the victim in supine position, face up.
2.   Face the victim; kneel, straddling the hips.
3.   Place one of your hands over the other, with the heel of the
     bottom hand on the abdomen, slightly above the navel, and below
     the ribcage.
4.   Press your hands into the abdomen with a quick upward thrust.

     When applying the Heimlich maneuver, be careful not to apply
pressure on the ribs. Such pressure may break the ribs of a child
or even of an adult.

CHOKING

Conscious Victim
     The following sequence of maneuvers should be performed imme-
diately and in rapid succession on the conscious victim in the sitting, standing, or lying position:

1.   Back blows--four in rapid succession administered between the
     shoulder blades. If ineffective proceed to 2.
2.   Manual thrusts--eight in rapid succession below the sternum.
     Proceed to 3.
3.   Repeat back blows and manual thrusts until they are effective
     or until the victim becomes unconscious.

Unconscious Victim
     If the victim is not breathing but can be ventilated, proceed
with mouth-to-mouth resuscitation.

If the victim is not breathing and cannot be ventilated, quickly perform the following sequence:

1. Back blows--four in rapid succession. If ineffective proceed to 2.
2. Manual thrusts--eight in rapid succession with victim lying on back. If ineffective proceed to 3.
3. Finger probe--Use your index finger and probe deep into the throat using your other hand to hold the mouth open wide. If unsuccessful proceed to 4.
4. Repeat sequence--persist.

ANIMAL BITES
Animal bites may cause punctures, lacerations, or avulsions. Not only do the wounds need care but consideration must be given to the possibilities of infection, including rabies and tetanus.
After the bite:

1. Keep the animal alive and make every effort to restrain the animal for observation.
2. If it is necessary to kill the animal, take precautions to keep the head free from damage.
3. Arrange for medical attention to the victim.
4. Immobilize the affected body part.
5. Wash the wound and the area around it with soap and water, flush the bitten area with water and apply a dressing.
6. Treat for traumatic shock.

BLISTERS
Blisters can result from friction or from burns. A broken blister must always be treated as an open wound.
Recommended treatment:

1. If all pressure can be relieved until the fluid is absorbed, blisters are best left unbroken.
2. Self-care for blisters should not be attempted when the blister fluid lies deep in the palm of the hand or sole of the foot.
3. Blisters resulting from burns should never be broken.
4. If friction blisters must be broken:
   a) Wash the entire area with soap and water.
   b) Make a small puncture hole at the base of the blister with a sterile needle.
   c) Apply a sterile dressing and protect the area from further irritation.

EYE INJURIES
Injury to the eyelid is much like other soft tissue injuries, and the first aid treatment is similar. A blunt injury or contusion often occurs from a severe direct blow as from a fist or in an

explosion. In serious cases, the structure of the eye may be torn or ruptured. Secondary damage may be produced by the effects of hemorrhage, and later by infection. Penetrating injuries of the eye are extremely serious. If an object lacerates or penetrates the eyeball, a loss of vision or even blindness can result.

Injury to the Eyelid
        Recommended treatment:

1. Stop hemorrhage by gently applying direct pressure.
2. Apply a sterile or clean dressing.
3. Seek medical assistance without delay.

Blunt Injury or Contusion
        Recommended treatment:

1. Apply a dry sterile or clean dressing.
2. Transport to the hospital with the victim lying flat.

Penetrating Injuries
        Recommended treatment:

1. Make no attempt to remove the object or to wash the eye.
2. Cover both eyes to lessen eye movement. Avoid making the covering so tight as to put pressure on the affected eye.
3. Keep the victim quiet.
4. Transport to the hospital immediately with victim lying down, face up.

RESPIRATORY EMERGENCIES
        A respiratory emergency is one in which normal breathing stops or in which breathing is so reduced that oxygen intake is insufficient to support life. The following may have occurred:

1. Breathing movements stopped.
2. Victim's tongue, lips, and fingernail beds blue, or perhaps cherry-red (in carbon monoxide poisoning).
3. Victim unconscious.
4. Pupils of the eye dilated.

Carbon Monoxide Poisoning
        Recommended treatment:

1. Ventilate area before attempting rescue.
2. Remove victim to fresh air.
3. Give all necessary first aid, including artificial respiration.
4. Recovery may be slow. It is often necessary to continue artificial respiration for a long time.
5. Treat for traumatic shock.

6. Get medical assistance as soon as possible.

Choking (Foreign body preventing breathing)
      Recommended treatment:

1. Try to manually clear the object from the victim's mouth using
   a sweeping motion of the index and middle fingers. Insert them
   inside the cheek. Slide them deeply into the throat to the
   base of the tongue, and out along the inside of the other
   cheek.
2. If breathing does not start immediately, try the Heimlich maneuver or Red Cross first aid procedures.
3. Treat for traumatic shock.
4. Get medical assistance if needed.

Electrical Shock
      Recommended treatment:

1. Cut off the power at the main switch before attempting a
   rescue.
2. Because electricity tends to paralyze muscles used in breathing, recovery time may be prolonged. Continue artificial respiration for a long time.
3. After breathing starts, treat for traumatic shock.
4. Care for any burns that may have resulted from the electrical
   shock.

WOUNDS
      A wound is a break in the continuity of the tissues of the
body, either internal or external. First aid for wounds includes
stopping bleeding immediately, protecting against infection, providing care to prevent traumatic shock, and obtaining medical assistance if needed.
      The loss of blood can cause traumatic shock. Loss of as
little as one quart of blood can result in loss of consciousness of
the victim. Because it is possible for a victim to bleed to death
in a very short period of time, any large, rapid loss of blood
should be stopped immediately.

Techniques to Stop Severe Bleeding

1. Direct pressure
   a) Place a thick pad of cloth over wound.
   b) Apply direct pressure by placing the palm of the hand over
      the dressing.
   c) The pad will absorb the blood and allow it to clot while the
      pressure slows the flow. (Do not disturb blood clots. If
      blood soaks entire pad, place another pad on top of the
      first.)

2. Elevation
   a) Unless there is evidence of a fracture, elevate a severely
      bleeding open wound of the hand, neck, arm, or leg. (Eleva-
      tion uses gravity to help reduce blood pressure in the in-
      jured area and thus aids in slowing the loss of blood.)
   b) Direct pressure must be continued.
3. Pressure on the supplying artery
   a) The use of the pressure point technique temporarily com-
      presses the main artery supplying blood to the affected part
      against the bone.
   b) If the use of a pressure point should be necessary, do not
      substitute its use for direct pressure and elevation, but
      use the pressure point in addition to those techniques.
   c) Use the brachial artery for the control of severe bleeding
      from an arm wound.
   c) Use the femoral artery for the control of severe bleeding
      from a leg wound.
4. Tourniquet.
         The use of a tourniquet is dangerous and should be a last
   resort. The decision to apply a tourniquet is in reality a decision to risk sacrificing a limb in order to save a life.
   a) The tourniquet should be at least 2 in. wide. Place the
      tourniquet just above the wound.
   b) Wrap the tourniquet band tightly around the limb twice and
      tie a half-knot.
   c) Place a short strong stick or similar object on the half-
      knot and tie two overhand knots on top of the stick.
   d) Twist the stick to tighten the tourniquet until bleeding
      stops.
   e) Secure the stick in place.
   f) Make a written note of the location of the tourniquet and
      the time it was applied and attach the note to the victim's
      clothing.
   g) The tourniquet should not be loosened except on the advice
      of a physician.
   h) The tourniquet should never be covered.

Prevention of Contamination and Infection
      Recommended treatment:

1. Wounds with serious bleeding
   a) The pad initially placed on the wound should not be removed
      or disturbed.
   b) Cover the wound and pad with a clean dressing.
   c) Transport the victim to medical assistance.
2. Wounds without severe bleeding
   a) Apply a dry sterile bandage or clean dressing and secure it
      firmly in place.
   b) Caution the victim to see a physician promptly if evidence
      of infection appears.

SUDDEN ILLNESS

First aiders often encounter emergencies that are not related to injury but come about from either sudden illness or a crisis in a chronic illness. Unless the illness is minor and brief, such as a slight dizziness, nosebleed, or headache, medical assistance should be sought.

Many persons suffering from heart disease, apoplexy, epilepsy, or diabetes carry an identification card or bracelet that contains information about the type of illness and the steps to be followed if the persons are found unconscious. Search the victim (in the presence of witnesses) for such identification.

Heart Attack

The signs and symptoms are: persistent chest pain, usually under the sternum (breastbone); gasping and shortness of breath; extreme pallor or bluish discoloration of the lips, skin, and fingernail beds; extreme prostration; shock; swelling of the ankles.

Recommended treatment:

1. Place the victim in a comfortable position, usually sitting up.
2. If the victim is not breathing, begin artificial respiration.
3. Treat for shock.
4. Get medical assistance.
5. Seek medical advice before transporting the victim.

Fainting

The signs and symptoms are: extreme paleness; sweating; coldness of the skin; dizziness; nausea.

Recommended treatment:

1. Leave the victim lying down.
2. Loosen tight clothing.
3. Maintain an open airway.
4. Give no liquids.
5. Unless recovery is prompt, seek medical assistance.

Epilepsy

The signs and symptoms are repeated convulsions--grand mal seizures. A milder form of epilepsy occurs without convulsions. There may be only brief twitching of muscles--petit mal seizures-- and momentary loss of contact with the surroundings (grand mal seizures are more common).

Recommended treatment:

1. Push away objects--do not restrain the victim.
2. Do not force a blunt object between the victim's teeth.
3. When jerking is over, loosen clothing around the victim's neck.
4. Keep the victim lying down.
5. Keep an open airway.

6. If breathing stops, give artificial respiration.
7. After the seizure, allow the victim to sleep or rest.
8. If convulsions occur again, get medical assistance.

BURNS
     A burn is an injury that results from heat, chemical agents,
or radiation. It may vary in depth, size, and severity.
     The goals of first aid for burns are to relieve pain, prevent
contamination, and treat for traumatic shock.

Thermal Burns--First and Second Degree
     The symptoms include redness or discoloration, mild swelling
or pain, development of blisters, wet appearance of the surface of
the skin.
     Recommended treatment:

1. Apply cold water, or submerge the burned area in cold water.
2. Apply a dry dressing if necessary. It will almost always be
    necessary in cases involving second degree burns.
3. Blisters should not be broken or tissue removed.
4. Preparations, sprays, or ointments should not be used on burns.
5. Treat for traumatic shock if necessary.

Thermal Burns--Third Degree
     The symptoms include deep tissue destruction, white or charred
appearance of skin, and complete loss of all layers of the skin.
     Recommended treatment:

1. Cover burns with thick, sterile dressings.
2. If hands are involved, keep them above level of the victim's
    heart.
3. Keep burned feet or legs elevated.
4. A cold pack may be applied to the face, hands, or feet but ex-
    tensive burn areas should not be immersed.
5. Adhered particles of charred clothing should be left in place.
6. Ointments, sprays, or other preparations should not be applied
    to burned areas.
7. Arrange for medical assistance and transportation to the hos-
    pital.

Chemical Burns of the Skin
     Recommended treatment:

1. Wash away the chemical with large amounts of water, using a
    shower or hose, as quickly as possible and for at least 5 min.
    Remove clothing from affected areas.
2. If first aid directions for burns caused by specific chemicals
    are available, follow them after the flushing with water.
3. Apply necessary dressings and get medical assistance.

Burns of the Eye
     Recommended treatment:

Acid burns:

1. Thoroughly wash the face, eyelid, and eye for at least 5 min.
    If the victim is lying down, turn the head to the side, hold
    the eyelid open and pour water from the inner corner of the eye
    outward.
2. If a weak soda solution (1 teaspoon of baking soda added to 1
    quart of water) can be made quickly, use the solution after the
    first washing of the eye with tap water.
3. Cover the eye with a dry, clean protective dressing. Cotton
    should not be used.
4. Get medical assistance.
5. Caution the victim against rubbing the eye.

Alkali burns:

1. Flood the eye thoroughly with water for 15 min.
2. If the victim is lying down, turn the head to the side. Hold
    the eyelid open and pour the water from the inner corner out-
    ward.
3. Remove any loose particles of dry chemical floating on the sur-
    face of the eye by lifting them off gently with sterile gauze.
4. Irrigation of the eye is not appropriate.
5. Immobilize the eye by covering it with a dry pad or dressing.
6. Get medical assistance.

POISONING

Poisoning by Mouth
     Recommended treatment:

General:

1. If victim is unconscious, keep the airway open, administer ar-
    tificial respiration if necessary, and transport as soon as
    possible to obtain medical assistance.
2. While giving first aid to the victim, have someone else get ad-
    vice by telephone from a doctor, hospital, or poison control
    center.
3. If vomiting is to be induced, do so by tickling the back of the
    victim's throat or by giving a nauseating fluid, such as syrup
    of ipecac or mustard and water.

If it is not known what poison the victim swallowed:

1. Dilute the poison with water or milk.

2. Try to find out what poison has been swallowed.
3. Get medical assistance immediately.

If it is known that the victim has not swallowed a strong acid, strong alkali, or petroleum product, but the original container is not obtainable:

1. Dilute the poison with water or milk.
2. Induce vomiting.
3. Get medical assistance immediately.

If you have the original container from which the known poison came:

1. Look for a specific antidote described on the label of a commercial product and administer it according to directions, if the victim is conscious.
2. Save the label or container.
3. Get medical assistance immediately.

If a strong acid is involved:

1. Dilute with 1 glass of water or milk.
2. Neutralize with milk of magnesia or other weak alkali, mixed with water--3 to 4 glasses for adults or 1 to 2 glasses for children.
3. You may find it necessary to administer milk, olive oil, or egg white as a demulcent to coat and soothe the stomach and intestines.
4. Get medical assistance immediately.

Poisoning by Plants
        The majority of skin reactions following contact with offending plants are allergic in nature and are characterized by the general symptoms of headache and fever, itching, redness, and a rash. Ordinarily, the rash begins within a few hours after exposure, but it may be delayed for 24 to 48 hours.
        Recommended treatment:

1. Remove contaminated clothing; wash all exposed areas with soap and water, followed by rubbing alcohol.
2. Apply calamine or other soothing skin lotion if the rash is mild.
3. Seek medical assistance if a severe reaction occurs, or if there is a known history of sensitivity.

Poisoning by Marine Life
        A variety of species of fish are equipped with venom apparatus attached to dorsal or other spines. Examples include catfish, weever fish, scorpion fish (including zebra fish), toadfish and surgeonfish. First aid treatment relates to the symptoms, since little is known regarding antidotes.

Stings from jellyfish and the Portuguese man-of-war produce a venom which in turn produces burning pain, a rash with minute hemorrhages in the skin, shock, muscular cramping, nausea, and respiratory difficulty.
Recommended treatment:

1. Wipe off affected area with a towel, and wash the area thoroughly with diluted ammonia or rubbing alcohol.
2. Give aspirin for pain.
3. Seek medical assistance if symptoms are severe.

Poisoning by Insects
    Stings from ants, bees, wasps, hornets, and yellow jackets can cause death due to allergic reaction.
    Spiders in the United States are generally harmless. However, black widow spiders and the brown recluse (violin) spider are poisonous and bites can be harmful. Medical assistance should be sought.
    Scorpions inject venom through a stinger in the tail. Fatalities have been recorded. Medical assistance is needed.

Severe reactions:
    Recommended treatment:

1. Give artificial respiration if indicated.
2. Apply a constricting band above the injection site on an arm or leg. Slip your index finger under the band when it is in place, and loosen band slightly. (The band should be removed after 30 min.)
3. Keep the affected part down, below the level of the victim's heart.
4. Apply ice contained in a towel or plastic bag, or cold cloths, to the site of the sting or bite.
5. Give aspirin for pain.

Poisoning by Venomous Snakes
    Recommended treatment:

1. Keep the victim calm and quiet. Transport victim to a source of medical assistance as quickly as possible.
2. Immobilize the arm or leg in a lowered position, keeping the involved area below the level of the victim's heart.
3. Treat for shock.
4. Give artificial respiration if needed.
5. Get immediate medical assistance.

CHECKLIST

1. Be aware of the available first aid courses.   _____
2. Know appropriate procedures to follow if a
   student is experiencing traumatic shock.   _____

3. Be able to administer artificial respiration. _____
4. Know the Red Cross and Heimlich maneuver proce-
   dures to use on choking victims. _____
5. Know what procedures to follow if students
   experience:
   Animal bites _____
   Eye injuries _____
   Poisoning _____
   Wounds _____
   Choking _____
   Fainting _____
   Burns _____

INDEX